T0250084

Managing Risk and Security in Outsourcing IT Services

Onshore, Offshore and the Cloud

Managing Risk and Security in Outsourcing IT Services

Onshore, Offshore and the Cloud

Frank Siepmann,

CISM, CISSP, ISSAP, NSA-IAM, NSA-IEM

CRC Press is an imprint of the
Taylor & Francis Group, an **informa** business
AN AUERBACH BOOK

CRC Press
Taylor & Francis Group
6000 Broken Sound Parkway NW, Suite 300
Boca Raton, FL 33487-2742

Contents

Foreword

I think that Frank does a great job of discussing outsourcing and his insights for areas to watch out for. He is dead-on with many of his observations, having been working with outsourced environments myself for a number of years. I appreciate his frank observations (pardon the pun!) and direct style in approaching the issues—in other words, he calls them as he sees them. The information on the different countries, albeit somewhat lengthy, provides a great perspective as to what is going on in the world and why it is so important to know who and what country you are dealing with. I also like the way that he moves into the cloud from outsourcing and shows the similarities. The latter section describing the controls, comments, and questions mapped to ISO27002-type requirements is very good as well. I also like the way that the book finished up with anecdotes to illustrate that these issues are real.

—Todd Fitzgerald
Global Information Security Director
Grant Thornton International, Ltd.

Preface

Since the early 1990s, outsourcing has had a large influence on various industries in the Western world. Outsourcing companies have attracted industry giants such as Ford, GE, and Siemens, just to name a few, with promises of better expertise and significant cost savings. Now approximately 20 years later, not all of those promises have been kept. Organizations have learned their lessons—outsourcing is not a silver bullet. Some political and economic dynamics have resulted in a shift in how outsourcing is perceived. One of the areas of concern with many outsourcing customers is the level of security and privacy of their data. Now with cloud computing becoming a standard in modern IT environments, the picture has become even fuzzier. Many security experts are raising the flag regarding security and privacy in outsourced cloud environments. This book was written with the intent to help the manager who is challenged with an outsourcing situation, whether preparing for it, living it day to day, or being tasked to safely bring back information systems to the organization. It provides guidance on how to ensure that security and privacy can be achieved during an outsourcing situation. I have worked in the consulting and outsourcing industry for more than 15 years, leading medium- to large-sized security organizations and teams. I learned over the years that many risks can be addressed when there is a much broader understanding of a situation than just the technical aspects.

Many factors can play into the success or failure of an outsourcing initiative. This book provides not only the technical background but also some broad information about outsourcing and its mechanics. Organizations sometimes try to resolve their issues of an expensive, fragmented IT infrastructure by looking into outsourcing. If this is truly a valid strategy, then it is heavily relying on circumstances and individual factors specific to that organization. Yet there are some common pitfalls that should be kept in mind before jumping to the conclusion that outsourcing will provide cost savings and a smoother-running operation. One critical factor for a smooth-running IT operation is a governance framework, resulting in mature processes, an executable IT strategy, and an IT environment that is maintainable. Most organizations that lack mature processes have to support an IT environment that ranges from Windows to three different UNIX flavors. Those environments are usually not sustainable in the long run, outsourced or not. To believe that outsourcing such an environment would result in cost savings and better performance can very quickly turn into a big disappointment. Yes, a large outsourcing company will certainly have the resources to support the various platforms and technologies. However, the more individuals an outsourcing company needs to provide to support a customer's environment, the higher the cost will be. Labor cost is the expensive part of the outsourcing equation, even delivered from low-cost countries like India and China. The leading outsourcing countries in particular have a common trend: the cost of living is rising, resulting in higher labor costs, making cost savings a short-lived dream.

That cost savings and security traditionally do not go hand in hand should be no surprise to anyone. Let's be clear: cost savings can be achieved in outsourcing if security is done right. However, the typical large-scale outsourcing engagement does not have security as the primary objective, but cost savings.

Definitions

This book uses for the purpose of standardization, whenever available, the definitions set by the US National Institute for Standards (NIST). Particularly in the fast-moving market of outsourcing, companies have come up with their proprietary marketing terminology, trying to distinguish themselves from their competitors. Looking under the "hood" of such proprietary offerings, they usually are easily tied back to the NIST definitions and standard industry terminologies.

Acknowledgments

I thank my family, friends, and former colleagues who have helped me to create this book.

1
OUTSOURCING

A precise definition of *outsourcing* has yet to be agreed upon. Thus, the term is used inconsistently across the industry. However, outsourcing is often viewed as involving the contracting out of a business function—commonly one previously performed in-house—to an external provider. In this sense, two organizations may enter into a contractual agreement involving an exchange of services and payments and it is called *outsourcing*.

History of Outsourcing

Nowadays there is a large number of outsourcing companies, ranging from small, employing a handful of people, to huge, employing sometimes more than 200,000 people. Whoever does business with a small outsourcing company has it easier in determining what they are dealing with than those doing business with the larger outsourcing companies. Most of them will have a large sales force that will make sure to paint the "right" picture of their services; however, it might not be a realistic picture. So what are some of the factors that can help to determine if an outsourcing company is the right one for the job? The history of a company can usually provide some pointers of its ability to operate the outsourced environment and if it has the right personnel to protect the valuable information that you entrust it with. Companies with large organic growth are usually a success story that is supported by satisfied clients and a workforce that brings the talent that you might be lacking in your own company. On the other hand are companies that have investors with deep pockets, supporting growth by acquisitions. This by itself is not bad; however, mergers and acquisitions are the reason that many organizations have underperformed or failed.* A half-integrated

---

* In 1997 a KPMG study referenced in *The Economist* (How mergers go wrong, July 20, 2000) showed that most postmerger companies underperformed.

organization can be more of a burden than a blessing. Due to the recent trend of insourcing, the market for outsourcing has seen smaller growth rates, resulting in takeovers and mergers. However, those new organizations lack in some cases the type of management that is required to successfully integrate the two companies—i.e., to achieve synergy between the entities of the new organization. Anyone who has worked for a small company and then for one of the larger companies knows the differences: in the smaller companies that lack specialists you find the "I do it all" mentality. The larger organizations, however, have adopted the "bring in the specialist" mentality, usually achieving better results. If a small company does not change its mentality as it grows, it will not perform well internally nor be able to provide the best service to its clients. Doing your research before making a decision on which company to use for outsourcing can result in a successful partnership instead of mediocre service that will cost you more in the end.

Early Days of Outsourcing

Outsourcing is nothing new, but it might have had a different name (*outsourcing* became the term for this in 1989; Mullins, 1996[*]). The concept of having another company to provide services for cost savings can be traced back to the 1950s and 1960s. Companies started moving away from the traditional model of the large integrated company that owns, manages, and directly controls its assets. In those years until maybe the 1990s, companies mainly used outsourcing as a tool to address skill needs that were not available within an organization. For example, publishers often used "outsourcing companies" for composition, printing, and fulfillment services. In the 1990s organizations began focusing more on cost saving measures by outsourcing functions that were necessary to run the company but not part of the core business. As the need for cost savings has increased over the recent years, more and more processes that are critical to an organization have been outsourced.

---

[*] Mullins, Rick. 1996. Managing the Outsourced Enterprise. *Journal of Business Strategy,* 17(4): 28–36.

Current State

In recent years since the late 1990s, there has been no general rule of how organizations handle outsourcing. There has been a general trend of outsourcing core processes (e.g., human resources) to outsourcing organizations. However, other organizations did a 180-degree turn and are bringing everything back in-house, minimizing the dependency on third parties. One of the key differentiators between the two groups of organizations is the agility of their business. Another is how leadership in an organization feels about their need to address challenges like repositioning the organization in the market place.

Delivery Models

The outsourcing industry has developed numerous delivery models, allowing for cost savings and attracting talent for low salaries in locations that have the necessary infrastructure to run an outsourcing operation.

Onshoring

Onshoring is often, wrongfully, defined as an overseas investment by a domestic company (or overseas affiliate) that is subsequently reinvested back into the domestic marketplace. In reality, onshoring has a broader definition and is actually defined as any direct investment into the domestic marketplace by a domestic company.

Nearshoring

Nearshoring and onshoring are very similar. The difference is that the investment does not necessarily go back into the domestic market but rather to a neighboring country (e.g., Mexico or Canada for US-based companies). With European countries this could mean that the investment takes place in the E.U. marketplace but not in the same country.

Offshoring

Offshoring describes the relocation of a business process from one country to another that is not necessarily a directly neighboring country (see "Nearshoring"). Offshoring has made up a large portion of today's outsourcing business models, achieving significant cost savings due to cheap labor in those outsourcing destinations.

Outsourcing Types

The outsourcing industry has been reinvented for decades. The latest invention is cloud services that have relabeled traditional services (e.g., Software as a Service being a prime example—now a cloud service model) to attract clients. Today there are two major outsourcing types: *technology outsourcing* and *business process outsourcing*. To reflect the variety in today's outsourcing offerings, some of the other outsourcing types are mentioned below.

Technology Outsourcing

Technology outsourcing (TO) is the older of the two main outsourcing types. It allows a client to use the technical capabilities of an outsourcing company for its purposes. Clients do not require the computing power in-house anymore; instead, the outsourcing company provides its IT systems and shares them across many clients so that a required dedicated solution can be provided to a client.

Business Process Outsourcing

Business process outsourcing (BPO) allows an organization to outsource complete business functions instead of just technology. An outsourcing company offering BPO can provide services like human resources to a client so that the client does not need to invest in skilled personnel and office space. BPO usually involves business processes that are outside the core competency of a company. However, there has been a trend to also outsource more and more core business processes. Models like Software as a Service (SaaS) provide the foundation for companies like Salesforce.com to offer fully automated solutions in the BPO space, making them great examples for business process outsourcing.

Business Transformation Outsourcing

Business transformation outsourcing (BTO) came up in the new millennium with some of the big players like IBM and Accenture offering BTO deals. Large organizations such as AT&T bought into these "co-sourcing" approaches. While not an actual joint venture, the normal structure for BTO deals aims to reward outsourcing companies for delivering ongoing innovation and cost savings. The new organization is usually a mix of both the client and outsourcing companies' personnel, having its own *pro forma* profit and loss and profit-sharing provisions.

Knowledge Process Outsourcing

Knowledge process outsourcing (KPO) is the fourth type of outsourcing that is becoming more common. It usually involves advanced research, analytical, and technical skills on the outsourcing company's side. The pharmaceutical research and development companies are great examples of an industry that makes use of this type of outsourcing. An example outside the pharmaceutical space is Motorola, which had the operating system for their famous Razr phone developed by a Brazilian company. This type of outsourcing usually involves short-term and peripheral projects.

The Internals of Outsourcing

Obviously there is not one operating model that maps to all outsourcing companies. However, there are similarities between the various outsourcing companies that are a result of their history and the drive to deliver cost-efficient services to their clientele.

The Phases

Outsourcing deals usually follow a six-phase life cycle:

1. *Strategy*—A company makes the strategic decision to outsource some or all of its IT or business operation.
2. *Selection*—The company starts a high-level selection on which outsourcing companies potentially could provide the services that are in scope for the outsourcing initiative. At a later state

of this phase a selection is made and an outsourcing company is chosen.

3. *Negotiation*—In this phase the negotiations start between the two companies. The outsourcing company might request additional information or send personnel to gather a first set of information to prepare for the implementation phase.

4. *Implementation*—During this phase the transitioning activities start in preparing for day one of the outsourcing operation. Usually the outsourcing company conducts interviews with client personnel, gathers more data, and revises financial estimates during this phase. Usually you will see the highest number of outsourcing personnel on-site, a mix between transition team and some early run-time team personnel during this phase.

5. *Management*—This is the phase where normal outsourcing operation starts (day one). The run-time team has taken on responsibility from the transition team and is providing the services in the scope of the outsourcing deal.

6. *Completion*—The final phase could mean that the outsourcing activities are transitioned back to the client or to another outsourcing company. This phase might never be executed if client and outsourcing company are both happy with the deal and keep extending it.

Typical Financial Outsourcing Model

Outsourcing IT or business processes creates an interesting symbiotic relationship between the outsourcing company and the client organization. Most of the times those symbiotic relationships are not completely understood by the client or the outsourcing company. Is it crucial for both sides to understand the financial model of the outsourcing deal, how it presents itself from the outsourcing company perspective or client side. So what are some of the typical financial characteristics of an outsourcing deal? Most of the IT outsourcing engagements are initially capital expenditures (CapEx) heavy for the outsourcing companies, with a return that increases over time as processes are optimized and further cost savings have been implemented. This maturity process is critical to the success of an outsourcing deal since the margins in today's outsourcing world are usually paper-thin and the profit is made by volume—more outsourcing engagements, more profit. BPO outsourcing deals are usually not as heavy on the CapEx but also follow a comparable life cycle when it comes to maturity and increased profit. This model by itself creates a difficult climate for security and privacy. In such cost-sensitive environments compliance is achieved mainly through service-level agreements (SLAs) and not risk management. The picture that the outsourcing industry likes to paint, claiming to be the experts for certain technologies or processes, is in most cases not what it really is. This is mainly due to the missing synergy between engagements. Most outsourcing companies create, for the purpose of mitigating business risks, stand-alone financial entities for their larger outsourcing engagements. These entities ("mini corporations") are expected to become cash-flow positive over time. Resources are hired into these mini corporations. Sharing resources across mini corporations is usually not done or in some cases not even an option.

Geographical Regions

Cost plays a significant role when it comes to personnel. As a result, large outsourcing companies have operations strategically located in key high-tech locations in many low-cost countries. This trend has gone so far that even traditional US outsourcing companies have, for example, more personnel in India than in the United States. When outsourcing to such offshore locations, it is important to understand the risks that the operation in that country has to manage, ensuring that the right decision is being made, allowing for a secure operation. Even with the best business continuity measures in place, it would be wrong to assume that an outsourcing company can operate in a "bubble" at an offshore location. Outsourcing personnel will need to commute between home and the office; systems require electricity; and nature's forces will not stop for an outsourcing company's facility either. The safety of your personnel that is visiting the offshore location is another critical factor to consider.

Nowadays you can find outsourcing companies in nearly any part of the world. Lately there is a trend to onshore and have service come from low-cost rural areas in the United States or Eastern Europe.

This trend is supported by the changes in how work visas are granted in the United States, making it more difficult for outsourcing companies to bring in low-cost resources to the United States.

Top Outsourcing Countries

Over the years some of the outsourcing countries have differentiated themselves from others. Global operating outsourcing companies want you to believe that they operate as one big global organization. The reality is that we are not all the same. So when you hear *global delivery model*, you might want to do your research on which countries are part of the global delivery model. In the end you will need to visit or at least have staff or auditors visit those locations. This section contains some information about the top 10 outsourcing countries* in 2012, evaluated in terms of six different aspects:

- *Society*—What are some of the key risk areas in the society? For example, religious groups and social and class differences are just some of the factors that are considered. This area is particularly interesting for the personal security of visitors.
- *Political*—Political stability ensures that your outsourcing partner stays in business and you do not suddenly lose your investment that is located in a foreign country due to political unrest or a change in ruling party. This area is particularly interesting when it comes to ensuring the continuity of operations.
- *Economy*—A healthy economy ensures growth and educated talent that the outsourcing company can use to support your operation. This aspect ensures that the outsourcing company stays competitive and provides quality service.
- *Crime*—A high crime rate is an indicator for many problems. It also puts your personnel at risk when traveling to that foreign country. Physical assets and intellectual property are particularly at risk in countries with high crime rates.
- *Environment*—You would not put your operation at risk by putting it in an area that is prone to hurricanes, earthquakes, or other natural disasters. Unfortunately, some of the

---

* As determined by Sourcing Line, an independent research firm.

top outsourcing countries are known for some of the biggest disasters in history. From a continuity of operations perspective, this is a critical risk area.

- *Infrastructure*—Does the infrastructure in the country ensure that the outsourcing company can operate seamlessly? Has the infrastructure kept up with the growth in the country? Your outsourcing company might have backup generators and uninterruptable power supplies, but if no diesel trucks can come to the facility, the operation will shut down within hours or days. If outsourcing personnel cannot come to work due to public transportation strikes (in many of the outsourcing countries, this is the main way to commute to/from work), then this will have an impact on the service provided to you.

Each country is given a rating based on a scale from 0 to 3, with 3 (dots) representing the highest risk and 0 (dots) representing an insignificant risk. The information used was obtained from the State Department* and from the CIA World Factbook.† Please refer to these two sources to get the latest information.

India

GDP est. (Official Exchange): $1.825 trillion (2012 est.)
Capital: New Delhi

---

* Please check http://www.travel.state.gov for updated information.
† Please check https://www.cia.gov/library/publications/the-world-factbook for the latest information.

Area (total): 3,287,263 sq km

Slightly more than one-third the size of the US

Data from *CIA World Fact Book* (https://www.cia.gov/library/publications/the-world-factbook/)

India has been the leading country for offshore outsourcing since the beginning of the offshore outsourcing trend. India has been the preferred choice for IT and BP outsourcing for organizations in the Americas and Europe for various reasons. IT and BP outsourcing first started in India in the mid-1980s due to its large English-speaking, low-cost workforce. India's outsourcing grew rapidly through the '90s, aided by the dot-com boom and the Y2K hype. Up to 2008 the growth was unprecedented; however, the growth rates have significantly dropped due to the global economic crisis and a disappointed Western-world customer base that is watching the record-setting corruption in India. Magazines like *The Economist* published many articles about this situation in India and how it impacts the growth in the country. One particular article, "In Search of a Dream,"[*] talks about the history and why the Indian government has to step up efforts to curb the corruption in the country, which has resulted in major deficiencies in the health and educational sectors. On the other hand, the fast growth of the outsourcing industry in India has resulted in an increase in certain forms of crime, ranging from falsifying educational records and resumes up to visa fraud.[†] According to experts,[‡] the general population of 1.2 billion (July 2013 est.) Indians are less than acceptable to opening up to Western culture, which would help to reform the country. Examples of this denial are strikes of various groups, such as local storeowners that have opposed Western chains opening stores in India. In July 2012 India was hit with one of the largest power outages in history. Over 620 million people in 20 states were without power due to a series of outages from the aging government-owned power grid. The overdrawing by states has been determined as the result of this massive outage.

India continues to experience terrorist and insurgent activities, which may affect Westerners. Anti-Western terrorist groups have

---

[*] http://www.economist.com/node/21563720/print

[†] http://www.justice.gov/usao/flm/press/2012/feb/20120215_Allala.html

[‡] http://www.economist.com/node/21563414

been active in India. Past attacks have taken place in public places, such as luxury and other hotels, trains, train stations, markets, cinemas, mosques, and restaurants in large urban areas. One of the more recent events is the February 13, 2012, bombing of an Israeli diplomatic vehicle near the diplomatic area in New Delhi. On September 7, 2011, a bomb blast at New Delhi's High Court killed 12 people; other attacks were the July 13, 2011, bombings of some crowded areas in Mumbai; the December 2010 bomb attack at Shitla Ghat in Varanasi during evening prayers; the February 2010 explosion at a café in Pune, Maharashtra; and several coordinated terrorist attacks in May 2008 in major cities throughout India. Noticeable are the November 2008 attacks in Mumbai where more than 170 people were killed, many of them Westerners. In late 2012 and early 2013, India got even more press for a series of rapes that in some cases resulted in women dying from their injuries. Rape of women has been a problem in India for decades. Some parts of the population are no longer tolerating that rapists are getting away without facing any consequences. Large demonstrations have resulted from this situation.

India has large religious ceremonies that attract hundreds of thousands of people, resulting in sometimes dangerous and often life-threatening stampedes. Some of the local demonstrations can begin spontaneously and escalate with little warning, disrupting transportation systems and city services, posing a risk to travelers. Indian authorities occasionally impose curfews and/or restrict travel to handle the situation. The northern city of Allahabad is home to one of the world's largest religious gatherings, which lasts 55 days and has more than 110 million people attending.

India still has its caste system that can result in tensions between the various castes and religious groups, causing disruption and violence. In many cases the demonstrators block roads near popular tourist sites to disrupt transportation and gain the attention of Indian authorities. Occasionally the vehicles transporting tourists are attacked.

India has "anticonversion" laws in some states, and acts of conversion sometimes trigger violent reactions from Hindu extremists. India has several areas of instability, and the Indian state of Jammu and Kashmir is one in particular. The Indian government prohibits foreigners from visiting certain areas. The India–Pakistan border is another area of instability. Both India and Pakistan maintain a strong military presence on both sides of the border. Both India and Pakistan claim an area of the Karakoram Mountain range. Incidents of violence by ethnic insurgent groups, including bombings of buses, trains, rail lines, and markets, occur frequently in the northeastern states. US government employees are prohibited from traveling to the states of Assam, Arunachal Pradesh, Mizoram, Nagaland, Meghalaya, Tripura, and Manipur without permission from the US Consulate in Kolkata. Restricted area permits are required for foreigners to visit certain Northeastern states (see the list of restricted areas, below.) Maoist extremist groups, or "Naxalites," are active in East Central India primarily in rural areas. The Naxalites have a long history of conflict with state and national authorities, including frequent attacks on local police, paramilitary forces, and government officials, and are responsible for more terrorist attacks in the country than any other organization. In February 2012, four officers of the Border Security Force were killed in an ambush by Communist Party of India–Maoist rebels in the Malkangiri district of Odisha. In March 2012 Naxalite guerrillas abducted four people including two Italian nationals from a remote area of southern Odisha. Naxalites have not specifically targeted Westerners but have attacked symbolic targets that have included Western companies and rail lines. Naxalites are active in a large swath of India from eastern Maharashtra and northern Andhra Pradesh through western West Bengal, particularly in rural parts of Chhattisgarh and Jharkhand and on the borders of Andhra Pradesh, Maharashtra, Madhya Pradesh, Uttar Pradesh, Bihar, West Bengal, and Odisha. Civil unrest is common in the south-central Indian state of Andhra Pradesh over the contentious issue of creating a separate state called Telangana within Andhra Pradesh. Certain parts of India are designated as restricted areas by the Indian government and require special advance permission to visit. These areas include the following:

- The state of Arunachal Pradesh
- Portions of the state of Sikkim
- Portions of the state of Himachal Pradesh near the Chinese border
- Portions of the state of Uttarakhand (Uttaranchal) near the Chinese border

- Portions of the state of Rajasthan near the Pakistani border
- Portions of the state of Jammu and Kashmir near the line of control with Pakistan and certain portions of Ladakh
- The Andaman and Nicobar Islands
- The Union Territory of the Laccadives Islands (Lakshadweep)
- The Tibetan colony in Mundgod, Karnataka

The quality of medical care in India can vary considerably depending on area. Medical care in larger cities can be comparable to Western standards, but adequate medical care is usually very limited or unavailable in rural areas. Dogs and bats can pose a high risk of rabies transmission in most parts of India. Tuberculosis is a rising problem. Depending on time of year and location visited, a malaria prophylaxis is recommended.

In most parts of India summers are very hot. The heat usually begins in April and continues till the beginning of October when the monsoon season starts. The peak temperatures are usually reached in June, with temperatures in the northern plains and the west reaching 45°C (113°F) and more. The first monsoons hit the country during the same period, beginning in early June at the Kerala coast and moving further inland from there. Sometimes these monsoon rains can be very heavy and cause floods and severe damage along the big rivers of India, Bramaputhra and Ganges. The plains in the north and the countryside of Rajasthan usually have a cold wave every year in December and January. The minimum temperatures could go below 5°C (41°F). In the northern high-altitude areas can get snow; on the other hand, in the northern mountains the summer months are only mildly warm. Typhoons are usually not a danger for India. The typhoon season starts in August and usually lasts till November with the east coast of India having the highest typhoon risk. In recent years (2012) some of the larger Indian cities have been suffering from severe air pollution (smog) that is a result of the uncompromised growth of the Indian industry.

Risk Factors					
Society	Political	Economy	Crime	Environment	Infrastructure
●	●	●	●●	●	●●

Indonesia

GDP est. (Official Exchange): $878.2 billion (2012 est.)
Capital: Jakarta
Area (total): 1,904,569 sq km
Slightly less than three times the size of Texas
Data from *CIA World Fact Book* (https://www.cia.gov/library/
   publications/the-world-factbook/)

Indonesia has been moving away from its traditional dependency on exports and restructuring its economy to meet the challenges of IT and IT-related services. As part of these efforts, Indonesia is continually liberalizing economic policies that support its outsourcing industry, which has a large footprint in the call center market. The Indonesian government has been implementing simplified processes for foreign investments, tax-deductible expenses, and the development of training and research programs. Indonesia comprises 17,508 islands and has a population of approximately 251 million (July 2013 est.). This makes it the fourth most populous country after China, India, and the United States. Its Muslim population is the largest of any country. It is made up of about 300 ethnic groups, mostly with European, Malaysian, Chinese, Arab, or Indian background. Indonesia has one of the largest economies in Southeast Asia and is one of the G-20 major economies. It is the only Southeast Asian member of the *Organization of the Petroleum Exporting Countries* (OPEC). Indonesia's government holds a heavy influence on the economy with many state-owned enterprises. The global economic downturn in 2010 has taken a significant toll on the country, and the rebound has been slow. Some contributing factors might also be that the country was heavily hit in the East Asian crisis in 1997–1998 and by the unrest in 2012 due to Muslims condemning the release of a movie in the United States that put the prophet Muhammed into a bad light.

Since 2005, the Indonesian police and security forces have disrupted a number of terrorist cells that carried out several bombings at various times from 2000 to 2009. Indonesia suffered its worst terrorist attack in 2002, when more than 200 foreign tourists and Indonesian citizens were killed in Bali. Deadly car bombs have exploded outside hotels and resorts frequented by Westerners in Jakarta and Bali in 2003 and 2005 as well as outside the Australian Embassy in Jakarta in 2004. In July 2009, Jemaah Islamiya (JI)-affiliated elements bombed two Western hotels in Jakarta, killing foreigners and 9 Indonesians, and injuring more than 50, including 6 US citizens. Since these attacks, Indonesia has effectively pursued counterterrorism efforts through legislation and law enforcement. In 2010, security forces arrested more than 100 individuals on terrorism-related charges. However, Indonesia still suffers from violence that is carried out with little or no warning.

Indonesia is located on the "Ring of Fire," which often results in severe seismic activity that can pose grave threats and disrupt daily life and regional air traffic. The Indonesian emergency response capabilities are limited, and Westerners should prepare for unforeseen emergencies when living or traveling in Indonesia.

Indonesia has been ranked #118 out of 174 countries listed by the Transparency International corruption index, which is the lowest ranking out of all top-10 outsourcing countries.

Crime has been a problem in a majority of the metropolitan areas in Indonesia. Crimes of opportunity such as pickpocketing and theft occur throughout the country. Indonesian police have noted an upward trend in burglaries and armed robberies in Jakarta resulting in an increase of 25 percent in 2010. Claiming to act in the name of religious or moral standards, certain extremist groups have, on occasion, attacked nightspots and places of entertainment. Most of these attacks have sought to destroy property rather than to injure individuals. International news events can sometimes trigger anti-American or anti-Western demonstrations.

Credit card fraud and theft are serious and growing problems in Indonesia, particularly for Westerners. Travelers who decide to use credit cards should monitor their credit card activity carefully and immediately report any unauthorized use to their financial institution. ATM cards have been skimmed and cloned, resulting in bank accounts being drained.

Indonesia's healthcare system generally can be rated far below US standards. Some routine medical care is available in most major cities;

however, it is advisable to leave the country and seek medical attention in countries providing better care.

Indonesia is actually split by the equator making it an entirely tropical climate. Temperatures average between 23°C (73.4°F) in the higher mountain regions, 26°C (78.8°F) in the inland and mountain areas, and 28°C (82.4°F) in the coastal plains. The relative humidity is high and ranges between 70 and 90 percent. Indonesia sees extreme variations in rainfall, which are caused by monsoons. June to September is considered the dry season, with December to March being the rainy season. Western Sumatra, Java, Bali, the interiors of Kalimantan, Sulawesi, and Irian Jaya are the regions of Indonesia with the highest rainfall, measuring more than 2,000 millimeters per year. Typhoons can hit Indonesia between September and December, resulting in rainstorms and heavy winds. Not every season has strong typhoons, and in some years only a few typhoons occur during the tropical storm season.

Risk Factors					
Society	Political	Economy	Crime	Environment	Infrastructure
●●●	●	●●	●●	●●	●●

Estonia

GDP est. (Official Exchange): $21.86 billion (2012 est.)
Capital: Tallinn
Area (total): 45,228 sq km
Slightly smaller than New Hampshire and Vermont combined
Data from *CIA World Fact Book* (https://www.cia.gov/library/publications/the-world-factbook/)

Estonia joined the European Union in 2004 as a revitalized nation that had formerly been under Soviet rule. The nation, with its population of approximately 1.2 million (July 2013 est.), has been known for adopting innovations and developments in information and communication technologies that have proven to be more successful than those in some more developed nations in Western Europe. Estonia became a North Atlantic Treaty Organization (NATO) member in 2004 and joined the Organization for Economic Cooperation and Development in December 2010. Estonia also introduced the euro currency in early 2011.

The country has been known for its authorities being vigilant in combating terrorism and other threats to security. There have been no noticeable incidents of terrorism directed toward foreigners in Estonia. Civil unrest is rarely a problem in Estonia; even large public gatherings and demonstrations may occur on occasion in response to political issues. Medical care in Estonia still falls short of Western standards. The best places for medical care are located in major cities like Tallinn, Tartu, and Pärnu. Many highly trained medical professionals are available; however, many hospitals and clinics still suffer from a lack of equipment and resources.

Estonia has been ranked #32 on the Transparency International corruption index.

The climate of Estonia is typical of northern European countries, with warm, dry summers and fairly severe winters. January is typically the coldest month, with daytime temperatures usually around –5°C (23°F). However, winter months can be much colder, with temperatures far below zero, about –20°C (–4°F) or lower. Heavy snowfall or even snowstorms are also possible and are not unusual during winter months. In general the weather is often breezy and humid due to the proximity of the Baltic Sea.

Risk Factors					
Society	Political	Economy	Crime	Environment	Infrastructure
		●	●	●	

Singapore

GDP est. (Official Exchange): $276.5 billion (2012 est.)
Capital: Singapore

Area (total): 697 sq km
Slightly more than 3.5 times the size of Washington, DC
Data from *CIA World Fact Book* (https://www.cia.gov/library/
publications/the-world-factbook/)

Singapore began its history as an international trading post when British settlers came to the area in 1819. The nation is approximately three times the size of Washington, D.C. Today, close to 100 percent of the population of approximately 5.4 million (July 2013 est.) live in an urban environment. Singapore has established a very successful free-market economy, showing high stability and a very high per capita gross domestic product (GDP). Probably the most significant element of the nation's GDP is its exports, which are made up of electronics, IT products, pharmaceuticals, and financial services. Despite the economic crisis early in the new millennium, the economy is growing at a double-digit growth rate. Singapore's business environment is attractive to foreign investors, and macroeconomic stability is at a level comparable to that in Canada. This is supported by a Transparency International corruption index rating that puts Singapore at #5, better than Switzerland (#6) and Germany (#13). The level of corruption in Singapore has been the best of any of the top 10 outsourcing locations.

Singapore's roadways are some of the best in the world, as is their electrical supply—both are ranked higher than those in the United States. Contract enforcement in Singapore is much easier than in other outsourcing locations.

Singapore is considered a small, stable, highly developed country with an elected parliamentary system of government and a population comprising 75 percent Chinese, 14 percent Malay, 9 percent Indian, and 2 percent others. English is widely spoken; criminal penalties are strict, and law enforcement is rigorous. In 2001 the Singaporean government uncovered a plot master-minded by Jemaah Islamiyah (JI), a terrorist organization with links to Al Qaeda. The plans were disrupted, and the JI organization in Singapore was largely wiped out. Extremist groups in Southeast Asia have been identified with the desire to conduct attacks against the government, private sector facilities, and locations where Westerners are known to congregate. Those terrorist groups do not distinguish between official and civilian targets.

Singapore has a very low crime rate; however, credit cards should not be removed from your sight nor the numbers given over the phone. Particularly, the use of a secure Internet connection for financial transactions is recommended.

In Singapore people can be arrested for jaywalking, littering, or spitting. Commercial disputes that may be handled as civil suits in other countries can escalate to criminal cases in Singapore and may result in hefty fines and sometimes even prison sentences. For vandalism offenses a court in Singapore might impose a caning sentence on the violator. Authorities in Singapore may also impose caning for other offenses. Singapore police have the authority to conduct random drug analysis on both residents and nonresidents. They do not distinguish between drugs consumed before or after entering Singapore, always applying local laws. US citizens have been surprised that they were arrested for violations that would not have resulted in arrests in the United States.

Judges in Singapore hear cases and decide sentencing without a jury. The government of Singapore does not provide legal assistance except in capital cases. Legal assistance may be available in some other cases through the Law Society of Singapore.

Singapore enforces the laws pertaining to the propriety of behavior between people and the modesty of individuals. The Singaporean law known as "outrage of modesty" is defined as an assault or use of criminal force on any person with the intent to, or the knowledge that it may, outrage the modesty of that person. The penalties for noncompliance may include imprisonment for up to 2 years, a fine, caning, or a combination thereof. Western men are sometimes accused of inappropriately touching other people, often women, resulting in their prosecution and punishment under this Singaporean law.

Singapore provides a good medical network with good doctors. The doctors and hospitals expect immediate payment for health services by credit card or cash. Most Western health insurances are not accepted. Recipients of health care might be the target for Ministry of Health auditors gaining access to private patient medical records without the consent of the patient, and in certain circumstances physicians may be required to provide information relating to the diagnosis or treatment without the patient's consent.

Singapore has had occasional outbreaks of mosquito-transmitted illnesses. If you visit Singapore during a pandemic, as experienced in the 2009 H1N1 pandemic, you should expect that the Singaporean government will put in place strict measures like screening in public facilities such as the airport, hospitals, and museums or quarantining individuals that might have been exposed to the illness.

Singapore's road and highway network is highly developed and well maintained. Public transportation and taxis are abundant, inexpensive, and reliable. Closed-circuit cameras monitor all major roads.

Singapore's climate does not vary in temperature or air pressure much, but it does in rainfall. Singapore's climate is tropical, with an annual average temperature around 28°C (82.4°F), with daytime highs of 35°C (95°F) and more, and lows around 20°C (68°F). The relative humidity is quite high and ranges between 70 and 90 percent. There is a monsoon season from December to March and a dry season from June to September. Typhoons can hit Singapore from July to mid-November, sometimes causing heavy damage, flooding, and erosion. Most typhoons in the region travel other routes and hit Singapore quite seldom.

Risk Factors					
Society	Political	Economy	Crime	Environment	Infrastructure
●				●	

China

GDP est. (Official Exchange): $8.227 trillion (2012 est.)
Capital: Beijing
Area (total): 9,596,961 sq km

Slightly smaller than the US

Data from *CIA World Fact Book* (https://www.cia.gov/library/publications/the-world-factbook/)

The People's Republic of China was established on October 1, 1949. With a population of approximately 1.3 billion (July 2013 est.), China is the world's most populous country. It is the world's fourth largest country in terms of territory. The political power is centralized with the Chinese Communist party. For the past 20 years China has been undergoing major economic and social changes.

China has been in the press for various issues that have arisen in the 2010s. Accusations of currency manipulations, stealing of intellectual property, and human rights violations are just the tip of the iceberg. China has a hard-working, well-educated workforce that sometimes is living in extremely poor living conditions, to just have work. The society looks very much like the society in Europe or the United States during the industrial revolution, when masses of people from rural areas found their way into factories in the cities. As history showed Europeans and Americans, change will not wait for long. Lately, more and more riots and even organized strikes have been observed in large Chinese corporations that are manufacturing for companies in the Western world, most notably Apple. Cases of slavery have been reported in which missing people were forced to work in coal mines, sometimes far away from where they were abducted. The Chinese government still maintains its big firewall, filtering the information that goes into or out of China. Early in the new millennium, the Chinese government added as an additional measure the installation of government-owned spyware on any new personal computer sold in China. Many things indicate that the Chinese government is actively involved in hacking Western computer systems. One notable case was the incident in April 2010 in which for 18 minutes a majority of US- and Canada-based Internet traffic was rerouted to go through Chinese Internet routers.

The government has a tight control over foreigners that are in the country. Whether traveling to or living in China, foreigners are required to register with the police within 24 hours of arrival in the country. Many areas of China are off limits to Westerners. These areas can be accessed only in organized travel groups.

China itself is such a huge market and will soon become the largest market, with over 1.3 billion consumers that could impact the biggest manufacturers and retailers in the world. However, China's large population does not necessarily provide a competitive advantage against the established outsourcing industry.

China and India are key countries used by the global sourcing industry. China's growth has resulted in some tension between these two countries, usurping a significant segment of India's outsourcing revenue year after year.

China's five major cities that provide the majority of its sourcing services are Beijing; Chengdu; Shanghai, known for providing product development, research and testing, and business analytics; Shenzhen, specializing in software, application maintenance, and development; and Guangzhou, known for its engineering services.

The recession in the 2010s has boosted China's service industry, including its sourcing market. The Chinese government has recognized an opportunity and has made significant policy changes to provide better financial support, subsidies, tax breaks, and intellectual property protection to companies located in 20 pilot cities, including Hangzhou, Suzhou, Xian, Shanghai, and Beijing, among others.

China's economy was revived during Deng Xiaoping's reign in China, after it had been demolished for decades due to foreign invasions. Deng focused on a free market–oriented economy that started changing the living standards of its citizens. It also led to China's rapid industrialization, which made it one of the most important economies in the world and a "returning superpower" in many ways.

China's GDP has increased tenfold since 1978, and in 2009 China's economy became the second largest in the world after the United States. However, the country still belongs to the low- to middle-income per capita group of sourcing countries when measured on purchasing power parity. In 2009, when the global crisis resulted in less demand for Chinese exports, making the country's economy vulnerable for the first time in many years, the government started to reform its economic policies and increase its domestic consumption to lessen the country's dependence on foreign exports.

Due to its rapid economic success, China is facing major challenges including environmental damage. High domestic savings rates and low domestic demand, corruption and legal economic violations, and a lack of adequate job growth for its migrants and new entrants to the workforce have created tension within the society.

As of 2012 China's total workforce is an estimated 780 million, the largest in the world. China has also an edge in language skills, especially in cities like Shanghai, where most of the engineers can speak Japanese and Chinese.

Since the fall of the Cultural Revolution, China's education system has been focused on modernization. China has the highest number of university graduates in the world every year.

The main language of the people is Standard Chinese or Mandarin. However, it is estimated that only 5 percent of China's population speaks English.

According to the International Telecommunications Union, there are around 22.2 Internet users for every 100 inhabitants in China. This puts China below average, although it has a higher ranking compared with India or the Philippines.

China has one the best road systems, with the United States, Chile, Canada, Malaysia, and Thailand being the top 5 countries worldwide. The supply of electric power is also one of the most reliable ones of the top 10 sourcing countries. On the other hand, China has a low per capita subscription rate, despite having one of the largest telecommunications markets in the world.

For most Westerners, China is a very safe country. Petty street crime and business disputes between Westerners and Chinese partners are the most common safety concerns when doing business in China.

Chinese security personnel watch foreign visitors and may place Westerners under surveillance. Hotel rooms, offices, cars, taxis, telephones, Internet usage, and fax machines may be monitored by audio and video. Personal possessions in hotel rooms, including computers, may be searched without consent or knowledge.

China usually does not have violent crimes; however, violent demonstrations can erupt without warning, and in the recent past there have been some fatal bombings and explosions, which could pose a threat to foreign visitors. The majority of the local incidents are related to disputes over land seizures, social issues, employment, environmental problems, or ethnic minorities. Some of those incidents have become large scale and involved criminal activity, including hostage taking and vandalism. In China, visitors should always take routine safety precautions by paying attention to their surroundings. Petty theft remains the most prevalent type of crime. Pickpockets target Westerners at sightseeing destinations, airports, markets, and stores. Typically passports and wallets are targeted, with most incidents involving items kept in back pockets, backpacks, or bags and purses swung over a shoulder or set down in a taxi, vehicle, restaurant, or shop.

Narcotics-related crimes and use are on the rise in China. Chinese law enforcement authorities have shown little tolerance for illegal drugs, and they periodically conduct widespread sweeps of bar and nightclub districts, targeting narcotics distributors and drug users. Westerners from various countries have been detained in such police actions.

The circulation of counterfeit currency is a significant concern in China. Cab drivers and businesses are a typical entry point of counterfeit currency into circulation. There have been cases of people receiving counterfeit bills from freestanding ATMs.

Westerners have been detained and deported for distributing religious literature. Chinese customs authorities have enforced strict regulations concerning the importation of religious literature, including Bibles.

Most Chinese people use cell phones for calls and text messaging. Vendors require identification from anyone purchasing a SIM (subscriber identity module) card, and the purchaser's identity is registered with the government. Internet access is widely available throughout China. Most hotels, even in remote areas, offer Internet access, often for a fee. Low-cost cyber cafes or Internet bars are widely available and are often open 24 hours a day. The government requires that you show your passport and that a photo is taken before access is granted. Many websites are blocked, including social networking sites such as Facebook, and all Internet activity is monitored.

Before entering into employment or a commercial contract in China, contracts should be first reviewed by legal counsel in the United States and in China. Many Westerners have reported difficulties in getting their contracts enforced by Chinese courts. Others have reported that they were being forced out of profitable joint ventures and unable to secure legal recourse in China. If a court order requires paying a settlement in a legal case, failure to make this payment may result in an exit ban, which will prohibit departure from China until payment is made.

China ranks #80 on the Transparency International corruption index and is comparable to Bulgaria which is ranked #75.

In civil business disputes in China, the Chinese government may prohibit you from leaving China until the matter is resolved under Chinese law. There are cases of Westerners having to stay in China for months and even years while their civil cases are pending. In some cases defendants have even been put into police custody to prevent them from trying to leave the country. Chinese businesspeople who may feel that they have been wronged by a foreign business partner may hire "debt collectors" to harass and intimidate the foreigner in hopes of collecting the debt. Businessmen have in some cases been physically detained as leverage during dispute negotiations.

Air pollution is a big problem in many cities or even regions of China. The types of pollution reach from particle pollution up to high levels of ozone, potentially resulting in significant health effects. Air quality can differ significantly between cities or between urban and rural areas.

The level of medical service and quality varies throughout China. In many places, doctors and hospitals require payment in cash at the time of service and may not begin treatment without payment or may discontinue treatment if it becomes obvious that you are unable to pay. In most rural areas, only rudimentary medical facilities are available, often with poorly trained personnel who have little medical equipment and medications available. Rural clinics are often reluctant to accept responsibility for treating foreigners, even in emergency situations.

In China medical rules, regulations, and conditions vary greatly throughout the country. HIV is a significant concern in China. An estimated quarter of a million people in China are infected with HIV, most of whom are not aware of their status. Tuberculosis is also an increasingly serious health concern in China, and for the first time in 10 years an outbreak of polio was reported in 2012.

The traffic in China can be described as chaotic and largely unregulated, and right-of-way and other rules are usually ignored. Even minor accidents can turn into violent fights with sometimes the bystanders asking for bribes to favor one or the other driver. The average Chinese driver has fewer than 5 years of driving experience. As a result, the rate of fatal traffic accidents is one of the highest in the world.

With China being one of the largest countries of the world, it is difficult to make a general statement about the climate. China spans multiple climate zones. The southeast coast of China has been subject to strong typhoons and tropical storms, usually from July through September. China is also a seismically active country, with earthquakes occurring throughout the country. Notable earthquakes include one in Qinghai in 2010, in which 3,000 people were killed, and a major quake in Sichuan in 2008, when more than 87,000 people died.

Risk Factors					
Society	Political	Economy	Crime	Environment	Infrastructure
●	●		●	●●	●

Bulgaria

GDP est. (Official Exchange): $51.02 billion (2012 est.)
Capital: Sofia
Area (total): 110,879 sq km
Slightly larger than Tennessee
Data from *CIA World Fact Book* (https://www.cia.gov/library/publications/the-world-factbook/)

Many Eastern European countries are now interesting places for outsourcing companies. In 2010 Bulgaria was the first European country to be included as one of the top outsourcing countries.

Located in the Balkans, in southeastern Europe together with Slovakia, Romania, and the Czech Republic, Bulgaria is particularly interesting for companies in neighboring European countries that want to nearshore.

During the glory days of the USSR, Bulgaria was known as the "Soviet Silicon Valley," and its software sector was heavily subsidized by the government. For many decades Bulgaria was a key supplier of software and hardware to the Soviet Union and other Eastern

European countries. This has resulted in over 40 years of experience in hardware, software, and electronic development.

Bulgaria is attractive due to a stable macroeconomic and political environment, competitive pricing, and a highly educated and qualified workforce.

Despite its now capitalist system, the country still has remainders of the communist system in place. This is one of the reasons why the bureaucracy can create quite a number of challenges to the private sector. Particularly start-up companies can run into bureaucratic hurdles that can result in significant delays. The judicial system requires improvement. Addressing irregularities in the legal system and shortening of court action processes are desperately needed changes.

In 2007 Bulgaria joined the European Union and experienced rapid economic growth, particularly in urban areas. Since 2008 growth has slowed down due to the financial crisis. Facilities for travelers are widely available, although infrastructure conditions can vary, and some facilities and services are not up to Western standards.

The Republic of Bulgaria had an estimated 7 million residents in July 2013 and is the 16th largest country in Europe. Key land routes from Europe to the Middle East and Asia go through Bulgaria. It shares borders with Romania, Turkey, Greece, Serbia, and Macedonia. The main language is Bulgarian, followed by Turkish and Roma. English is the primary language used for international business transactions, and approximately 15 percent of the population speaks English fluently. The main religion is primarily Bulgarian Orthodox, with a smaller portion of the population being Muslims and Christians.

The World Bank has classified Bulgaria's open free-market system as an "upper-middle-income economy."[*] It is ranked as the lowest-income state member of the EU. However, it is one of the fastest-growing European countries in recent years.

Bulgaria became a People's Republic in 1946 after entering the Soviet bloc. After having its first multiparty elections in 1990 the country gained independence. Since gaining its independence and emerging as a parliamentary democracy, Bulgaria had to deal with inflation, unemployment, and corruption. In 2004 the nation joined NATO. After entering the EU, Bulgaria's economy grew at a rate greater than 6

---

[*] http://www.worldbank.org/en/country/bulgaria

percent due to the foreign investments and consumption. The government has been instrumental in driving reform and financial planning. During the global downturn starting in 2009, the economy contracted nearly 5 percent. In 2012 Bulgaria's workforce consisted of more than 3.4 million workers. Bulgaria has suffered a high unemployment rate. In 2012 the rate was at 9.2 percent. In 2012 approximately 70 percent of the total population lived in urban areas. Its largest city and capital is Sofia, with a population of 1.192 million people (2012).

Due to the euro crisis and the generally slow international economy, the country's unemployment rate has been going up. The situation was further exacerbated by the corruption of some of Bulgaria's public officials, the presence of organized crime, and a weakened judiciary system.

Bulgaria has a good education system. Many of Bulgaria's youth have completed higher education and previously have gone through intensive training in languages, sciences, and other technical subjects at a very young age.

Bulgaria has heavily invested in technology since breaking away from the USSR bloc. However, Bulgaria has low levels of Internet accessibility, one of the lowest of all EU member countries. In 2010 just one in three residents had access.

Economic competitiveness and stability are key aspects to the long-term security of an outsourcing business. According to the World Economic Forum,* which publishes the Global Competitive Index, Bulgaria is at the bottom of the index. The macroeconomic stability is being ranked above average, putting Bulgaria at number 9 among the top 10 countries. This makes it one of the countries with the most stable government surplus or deficit, national savings rate, inflation, interest rate spread, and government debt.

The quality of roads affects employees' productivity and companies' costs by adding to transportation cost of goods or damaging sensitive goods during transport. A study by the World Economic Forum ranks Bulgaria at the bottom in terms of road quality, together with other European countries such as Ukraine, Poland, and Romania. The reliability of the electrical supply is ranked low. Bulgaria, together with India, Pakistan, Vietnam, South Africa, and Argentina, are on the bottom of the list of countries with reliable electrical supply.

---

* http://www.weforum.org/issues/global-competitiveness

Being able to enforce contracts is critical to protect your investment in a foreign country. In Bulgaria it takes significant time and steps to enforce contracts, which puts it at the bottom of this list together with Indonesia, Egypt, Brazil, India, and Pakistan.

Bulgaria ranks below average for intellectual property protection as compared with Canada, the United States, and South Africa. This score goes hand in hand with the protection against software piracy.

Bulgaria's joining the European Union has enhanced its overall security environment for business travelers. Still, violence related to criminal groups can occur sporadically in public locations. Some of the incidents include bombings and shootings, likely the result of gang wars between rival organized crime syndicates. This remains a huge problem in Bulgaria's largely cash economy. In January 2010 a journalist who had published a book about Bulgarian organized crime was assassinated in Sofia in broad daylight.

Public protests in the form of demonstrations or strikes can occur sporadically, resulting in traffic disruptions, particularly in the center of cities. While these demonstrations are usually peaceful, confrontational demonstrations have occurred, and even demonstrations intended to be peaceful have turned into violent confrontations. Nationwide demonstrations in October 2011 resulted in some violence and destruction of property.

Particularly in crowded places, pickpocketing and purse snatching have been frequent occurrences. Con artists operate frequently on public transportation and in bus and train stations.

Automobile theft is a huge concern in Bulgaria; particularly four-wheel-drive vehicles and late-model European sedans are popular targets. The recovery rate of stolen vehicles is extremely low. Break-ins with cars are common in residential areas or near parks. Residential burglaries are also a common occurrence especially in major cities in Bulgaria. The installation of window grills, steel doors with well-functioning locks, and alarm systems is common in Bulgaria.

Making credit card charges over the Internet can be dangerous in Bulgaria.

Due to the potential for fraud and other criminal activity, credit cards are used sparingly and with extreme caution. It is not unusual for skimming devices surreptitiously attached to ATMs by criminals to be used to capture card numbers and personal identification numbers (PINs) for later criminal use.

Corruption remains an important concern of the Bulgarian government. Bulgaria was ranked #75 by the Transparency International corruption index. In comparison, Estonia was ranked #32. The Commission for Coordinating of the Activity for Combating Corruption manages the efforts of each government agency's internal inspectorate in fighting public corruption and engages in public awareness campaigns.

Bulgarian physicians are trained professionals with very high standards. Most hospitals and clinics, especially in village areas, are generally not equipped and maintained to meet US or Western European standards. Basic medical supplies like over-the-counter or prescription medications are widely available; however, highly specialized treatment may not be obtainable. The increasing number of cases of tuberculosis is becoming a serious health issue in Bulgaria.

To enter Bulgaria you might have to show evidence of valid health insurance. In many places within Bulgaria doctors and hospitals still expect payment in cash at the time of service.

A number of roads in Bulgaria are in poor condition and require repair. Rockslides and landslides may be encountered on roads in mountainous areas and contribute to the overall bad picture of road safety. During the agricultural season, livestock and animal-drawn carts are present, creating road hazards throughout the country. The travel conditions worsen during the winter season as roads become icy and potholes proliferate.

Driving in Bulgaria can be extremely dangerous. Aggressive driving habits and the lack of safe infrastructure with a mixture of late-model and old cars on the country's highways are the main contributing factors to a high fatality rate in road accidents. In particular, drivers of late-model sedans are known to speed and drive dangerously. The drivers of such vehicles are sometimes armed, organized crime figures.

Bulgaria's climate can be described as a temperate-continental with moderate variations, which is characteristic for Central Europe. Hot summers, long and cold winters, and very distinct seasons are typical for Bulgaria. Snow may occur throughout December to mid-March. In the mountainous areas of Bulgaria, snow is typical in those months.

The annual average temperatures can range from 8°C (46.4°F) in the north and 11°C (51.8°F) in the south, with temperatures of

2.6°C (36.68°F) in the mountains and 12°C (53.6°F) in the plains. The warmest areas are in the south of Bulgaria, which is influenced by the nearby Mediterranean Sea. Daytime temperatures can vary from 0°–5°C (32°–41°F) in the winter and 25°–30°C (77°–86°F) in summer months. The southern part of Bulgaria can be warmer than the northern and eastern mountainous areas. Particularly the Balkan Mountains can be cooler, with moderate daytime temperatures and cold nights in the summer and temperatures far below the freezing point in the winter.

The annual average rainfall is about 700 mm, more in the mountains (up to 1,000 mm and more) and less at the coast (around 400–600 mm). Typically it can rain throughout the year. In the summer, showers and thunderstorms are common, especially in the mountain areas. However, the winters are usually dry.

Risk Factors					
Society	Political	Economy	Crime	Environment	Infrastructure
	●	●●	●●		●●●

Philippines

GDP est. (Official Exchange): $250.4 billion (2012 est.)
Capital: Manila
Area (total): 300,000 sq km
Slightly larger than Arizona
Data from *CIA World Fact Book* (https://www.cia.gov/library/publications/the-world-factbook/)

The Philippines is known for its business process outsourcing capabilities, both in call center services and the nonvoice sector. It is considered an emerging player in the IT services market (web design, software development, application maintenance, etc.).

When outsourcing to the Philippines, expect strong English-speaking skills and awareness of Western business culture. In 2006, Philippine offshore outsourcing (IT and BPO) was about $3.3 billion; it has grown more than 30 percent per year to an estimated $9 billion in 2009 and is continuing to grow. Philippines is one of the veterans in outsourcing, first starting in the 1990s but really growing in earnest by the early 2000s. In 2004 the industry was only about $1.5 billion but grew almost 50 percent for several years and then 30 percent till 2009. Many of the older outsourcing operations are located in the capital city of Manila, but there has been growth in other cities such as Cebu City, Pasig City, Quezon City, and Mandaluyong City.

The Philippines has a population of approximately 106 million (July 2013 est.) and is one of the 10 largest outsourcing countries. However, the territory is less than one-tenth the size of China. The Philippines is a representative democracy with national elections taking place every 6 years.

The Philippines' growth averaged 5 percent from 2001 on, till in 2007 the economy accelerated and grew at 7 percent. Starting in 2008 the economic growth slowed down tremendously to 3.8 percent, mainly the result of the worldwide economic downturn. Even though the economy has had significant growth rates, it still faces a number of long-term challenges due to poverty and uneven income distribution.

The Philippines has the third largest English-speaking population in the world and has one of the highest literacy rates in the region.

The Philippines has a moderate competitiveness scoring on the Global Competitive Index. The Macroeconomic stability in the nation is considered high, even higher than in the United States.

Infrastructure in the Philippines is a major problem. The electric supply standard is well below Western standards, indicating significant problems with the generation and supply of electricity.

The Philippines is generally not an easy place to operate a business, ranking globally low when it comes to starting, registering, or filing taxes for a company. The Philippines' high level of corruption can often lead to unforeseen costs and lower efficiency in the workplace.

The Philippines was ranked #105 by the Transparency International corruption index. This ranking makes it the 2nd worst ranked country, out of the top-10 outsourcing countries, on the index. Only Indonesia was ranked worse at #118. The level of protection for intellectual property is generally low, and software piracy is high, much higher than in the United States or Singapore.

The Philippines has to deal with terrorism; the southern island of Mindanao and the Sulu Archipelago are of particular concern. Terrorist groups such as the Abu Sayyaf group and Jemaah Islamiyah, as well as groups that have broken away from the more mainstream Moro Islamic Liberation Front or Moro National Liberation Front, have carried out acts of terror, involving bombings resulting in deaths, injuries, and property damage. Gangs that kidnap for ransom operate throughout the Philippines and have targeted foreigners, including Filipino-Americans. Particularly in Sulu Archipelago, where foreigners have been kidnapped in 2009–2012, the security of foreigners is a concern.

Manila is an area with high crime where travelers, typically during a meal, may be given a substance that knocks them unconscious. They are then robbed of valuables, including their ATM cards, which are then used to drain their bank accounts. Kidnappings and violent assaults do occur in the metropolitan Manila area. There have been several instances of travelers arriving at the Manila international airport where shortly after they leave the airport area in a taxi or private vehicle, their vehicle is stopped, typically by an intentional rear-end collision, and the travelers are robbed.

One common form of credit/ATM card fraud involves the illicit use of an electronic device that retrieves and records information, including the PIN, from a card's magnetic strip. The information is then used to make unauthorized purchases. The Philippine Banking Association has warned the public that criminals sometimes attach electronic scanners to ATM card receivers; the scanners are designed to illicitly retrieve and record information from the credit/debit card's magnetic strip.

People violating the Philippines' laws, even unknowingly, may be expelled, arrested, or imprisoned. Penalties for possession, use, or trafficking in illegal drugs in the Philippines are severe, and convicted offenders can expect long jail sentences and heavy fines.

The Philippines offers adequate medical care in major cities, but even the best hospitals may not meet the standards of medical care, sanitation, and facilities provided by hospitals and doctors in most Western countries. Medical care is limited in rural and more remote areas.

The majority of hospitals require a down payment of estimated fees in cash at the time of admission. There have been cases of public and private hospitals withholding lifesaving medicines and treatments for nonpayment of bills. This can go as far as hospitals refusing to discharge patients or release important medical documents until a bill has been paid in full.

In 2011–2012 there were outbreaks of dengue and schistosomiasis in the Philippines. Schistosomiasis is transmitted by waterborne larvae. It is endemic in the Philippines, and there have been outbreaks in the Leyte area, as well as Mindanao, Bohol, Samar, and the provinces of Sorsogon (the southern tip of Luzon Island) and eastern Mindoro Island. There is an increased risk of dengue fever and malaria. Tuberculosis is also an increasingly serious health problem there.

With over 7,000 islands making up the Philippines (only 800 being inhabited), road conditions play an important role. The quality of the roads can vary significantly but is quite low, falling well below Western standards, to a level that is comparable to Russia and many of the other former Soviet states. Travel within the Philippine archipelago can be done by boat, plane, bus, or car. In general, drivers in the Philippines are less disciplined than those in most Western countries. Between 2009 and 2012 there have been nine major interisland ferryboat accidents, with eight causing significant loss of lives. There have also been serious bus accidents due to poor bus maintenance.

The Philippines' main climate variable is rainfall. It is a tropical climate with the coastal plains averaging year-round temperatures about 28°C (82.4°F) and relative humidity that ranges between 70 and 90 percent. There are extreme variations in rainfall, which are linked to monsoons. June to September is the dry season, and December to March is the rainy season. Western and northern parts of the Philippines experience the most precipitation. Typhoons can hit the Philippines from July to mid-November and have caused heavy damages, flooding, and erosion.

Risk Factors					
Society	Political	Economy	Crime	Environment	Infrastructure
●●	●	●	●●	●●	●●

Thailand

GDP est. (Official Exchange): $365.6 billion (2012 est.)
Capital: Bangkok
Area (total): 513,120 sq km
Slightly more than twice the size of Wyoming
Data from *CIA World Fact Book* (https://www.cia.gov/library/publications/the-world-factbook/)

Thailand is a famous tourist destination; however, it is fast becoming a dominant player in the information technology industry. It has ranked in the top outsourcing countries since 2010.

In 1996 Thailand launched its first IT policy, called the IT 2000. The national IT policy was the second phase of the project. It covers a period of 10 years, and its main goals are to increase the number of knowledge workers and knowledge-based industries in five key areas: e-society, e-education, e-industry, e-commerce, and e-government.

Thailand's IT and BPO industries have managed to make a name in the fields of database management outsourcing, COBOL programming, animation or digital content sourcing, medical, and biometric-related services.

Thailand's government wants the country to be ranked in the top three countries for outsourcing by the end of 2013. This is not very likely to happen. Thailand has yet to make a full and dynamic economic recovery to regain the confidence of its consumers and business investors. Although Thailand has admirably held the outsourcing/offshore industry fairly well, its economy hasn't reached its fullest potential yet, due to the continuing political instability that is plaguing the country.

Among the population of approximately 67 million (July 2013 est.) there is a high literacy rate, though Thailand has never been colonized and the teaching methods used are heavily dependent on rote rather than student-centered techniques. Education is a relatively new term for the people. Improving the standards of the educational system has been challenging. Only well-educated and wealthy people speak English; the majority of the people are not proficient in English. However, most Thais working in businesses dealing with foreigners can speak at least some level of English.

The country's main source of income has been exports, which accounted for more than two-thirds of its gross domestic product in the past. Due to the global financial crisis of 2008–2009, this sector has been significantly impacted, resulting in double-digit drops in most industrial sectors. As a result the government has been focusing on domestic infrastructure projects, foreign business investments, and outsourcing to stimulate and revive the economy.

Thailand is the only Southeast Asian country untouched by European power. Thailand is governed by a constitutional monarchy. It adopted its current constitution following an August 19, 2007, referendum. Approximately 95 percent of the population is of Thai descent. Its main religion is Buddhism, followed by Islam and then Christianity. Thailand is one of the countries that poses a continued risk of terrorism in Southeast Asia.

The political environment in Thailand shows deep political divisions. Protesters holding political rallies frequently voice their opinions. Between March and May 2010 several political protests throughout Thailand took place, resulting in at least 91 deaths and injuries to more than 260 people. Political demonstrations are frequent events in Thailand, with many being scheduled on the anniversary of political events and others happening with little warning. Demonstrations can attract tens of thousands of participants and often cause severe traffic disruptions, especially if they include processions from one site to another.

The further south you go in Thailand, the higher the rate of daily incidents of criminally and politically motivated violence, including incidents attributed to armed local separatist groups. Be aware that Thai authorities have occasionally instituted special security measures in affected areas, such as curfews, military patrols, or random searches of train passengers.

The Thailand–Burma border is a site of an ongoing conflict between the Burmese army and armed opposition groups, as well as fights between Thai security forces and armed drug traffickers.

In general the crime rate in Bangkok and other Thai cities is lower than that in many US cities; crimes of opportunity such as pickpocketing, purse snatching, and burglary are very common.

In 2011–2012 there have been some crimes against Westerners, including the murder of several independent travelers on the southern islands of Phuket and Ko Samui.

Tuk-tuk and taxi drivers are organized and have been described in media reports as being like a "mafia." Particularly when it comes to alternative transportation services, they have organized blockades on van and bus services.

There have been reports of prostitutes or bar workers drugging people with powerful sedatives in order to rob them. Westerners have been no exception and have also been victimized by drugged food and drink, usually offered by a friendly stranger who is sometimes posing as a fellow traveler on an overnight bus or train.

Some foreigners have been victimized by criminals presenting themselves as police, sometimes even wearing police uniforms.

In Thailand the king and the royal family are held in the highest regard, and tarnishing the image of the royal family is a serious criminal offense that is punishable by a prison sentence of 3 to 15 years. Thai authorities actively search for and investigate Internet postings, including blog entries and links to other sites. Westerners have been arrested for offensive actions that occurred outside of Thailand.

The Thai government has repeatedly stated that it will not tolerate any group trying to overthrow or destabilize the governments of nearby countries. This has resulted in many US citizens who were suspected of advocating the armed overthrow of governments being "blacklisted" from entering the country.

Thailand has a death penalty for severe drug offenses. The police regularly raid discos, bars, or nightclubs, looking for underage patrons and drug users.

In 2010, there were several news reports that duty-free store employees in league with police at airports had added unpurchased items to foreigners' check-out bags or did not charge for all the items purchased. This resulted in the police then stopping the foreigners as they exited the stores and charging them with shoplifting.

The importation of medicine for personal use is allowed as long as the amount is less than a 30-day supply.

Traveling by ferry, air, bus, or rail during periods of heavy rain usually requires a check with the transportation company ahead of time to ensure that its service is still operating. If you are driving, roads might not be passable during heavy rain. In Thailand ferries and speedboats are used for transportation to and from the many islands off the Thai mainland and along rivers. Those ferries and speedboats are often overcrowded and do not carry sufficient safety equipment onboard.

Many car and motorbike rental companies require the passport of the driver as a deposit. In case of damage to the rental vehicle, the passport is held until the damage has been paid for. When purchasing insurance from the rental company, a receipt showing you paid for insurance is advisable.

Traffic accidents, minor property damage, and petty crimes are often settled through informal arbitration at a police station, with the police as arbiters or sometimes as participants. It is a traditional way of settling a dispute that Thais prefer, to avoid legal formalities and a lengthy court process. If parties cannot come to a compromise or one of the parties declines to participate, the police then will write a report and the formal judicial process begins.

Thailand was ranked #88 by the Transparency International corruption index, putting it above India, which was ranked #94.

Medical treatment facilities are generally adequate in Thailand's urban areas. In Bangkok, Chiang Mai, and Pattaya, good facilities exist for routine, long-term, and emergency health care. Basic medical care is available in rural areas, but English-speaking providers are rare in those areas. There is increasing concern about counterfeit medications in Southeast Asia, and it is recommended to purchase medication only from international chain pharmacies.

Dengue and chikungunya are viral infections transmitted via mosquitoes. These infections are endemic in Thailand and can make a person very ill and even result in death. HIV and AIDS are epidemic in Thailand. Heterosexual transmission accounts for most HIV infections, particularly among prostitutes of both sexes, as well as among injected-drug users. According to the World Health Organization (WHO), pandemic influenza has been confirmed with human cases of the H1N1 (swine flu) and the H5N1 (bird flu) strains of influenza in Thailand. Tuberculosis is on the rise and becoming a serious health concern in Thailand.

Another area of concern is the poor air quality in Chiang Mai and other areas of northern Thailand, posing a health threat during the dry season of the year.

In Thailand, traffic moves on the left side of the road, although motorcycles and motorized carts often drive against the traffic flow on the right. Many pedestrians have been killed or seriously injured while crossing the street. Traffic accidents are common in Thailand. The accident rate is particularly high during long holidays, when alcohol use and traffic are both heavier than normal. During Songkran (the Thai New Year) holiday celebrated in April, the traffic problems worsen due to people throwing water at passing vehicles as part of their traditional celebration. Thailand's major cities are connected through paved roads, many of which have four lanes. Speeding, reckless driving, passing, and failing to obey traffic laws are common in most regions of Thailand. Commercial drivers commonly consume alcohol, amphetamines, and other stimulants on the job.

The scarcity of ambulances and the congested roads make it nearly impossible for accident victims to receive timely medical attention. Thailand requires that all vehicles have third-party liability insurance for death or injury. However, there is no requirement for property damage insurance coverage. Bangkok has an extensive bus system; however, buses are usually overcrowded and are often driven with little or no regard for passenger safety. In conjunction, privately operated vans, which are not regulated, carry 8–15 passengers within Bangkok and to and from other cities. Other cities typically have only limited public transportation and usually do not have metered taxis. In many cases, motorcycle taxis, tuk-tuks, bicycle-powered rickshaws, and pickup trucks will be the only options available for travelers without their own transport.

Thailand's climate is best described as a tropical monsoon climate with strong monsoon influences, a considerable amount of sun, a high rate of rainfall, and high humidity that makes it sometimes feel quite uncomfortable. There are two seasons in Thailand: a dry period in the winter and a very humid rainy period in the summer. The year-round temperatures range between 22°C (71.6°F) and 27°C (80.6°F).

Risk Factors					
Society	Political	Economy	Crime	Environment	Infrastructure
●●	●	●	●	●	●

Lithuania

GDP est. (Official Exchange): $42.16 billion (2012 est.)
Capital: Vilnius
Area (total): 65,300 sq km
Slightly larger than West Virginia
Data from *CIA World Fact Book* (https://www.cia.gov/library/
  publications/the-world-factbook/)

Lithuania is considered stable from a political and economic perspective. It offers geographical proximity to (European) clients, a quality infrastructure, and an educated workforce. Among all Baltic nations, Lithuania has the largest IT industry, with a presence of nearly 75 percent of all Baltic IT companies. Lithuania gained its independence following World War I, but was soon annexed by the USSR in 1940. By 1990, after the fall of the Soviet Union, Lithuania declared its independence as one of the first nations. Lithuania offers most amenities that Westerners are used to. However, in some parts of the country, some of the goods and services taken for granted in other countries may not be available.

Due to efforts to restructure its political and economic environment, aiming to ensure integration to Western European organizations, Lithuania has been a member of NATO and the European Union (EU) since 2004. The country is a relatively small nation about the size of West Virginia, with a population of approximately 3.6 million (July 2013 est.).

Lithuania's economy is heavily dependent on trade with Russia. Many large companies in Lithuania are private or are in the process of privatization, such as utility companies. The economy has been slowly recovering after losses of up to 14 percent in the years around the global recession. Lithuania's economic competitiveness is considered very high, and its macroeconomic stability is strong.

The literacy level in Lithuania is very high; virtually 100 percent of Lithuanian adults can read and write. The official language is Lithuanian, but schools teach English, French, and German as the primary foreign languages. In 2001, 54 percent of students were learning English, up from nearly 10 percent five years prior.

Internet connections in Lithuania are among the fastest in the world, and quality of Internet service is among the best also.

While the quality of electrical supply is lower than that in the United States, it still ranks above most nations, particularly the neighboring Eastern Europe countries.

Compared with its neighboring Eastern European countries, Lithuania has less of a problem with corruption. However, corruption can be part of doing business in Lithuania, which was ranked #48 by the Transparency International corruption index.

The protection of intellectual property can be an issue, with Lithuania scoring at the same level as Poland, India, or Indonesia. Particularly software piracy is much higher than in other countries, but still considered only moderately high.

Lithuania has few to no civil disturbances. Sometimes marches and protests do occur in larger cities. On occasion, foreigners have been subject to violent crimes, such as muggings, or have become involved in altercations with inebriated individuals. There have been rare cases of racially motivated verbal and sometimes physical harassment of foreigners or ethnic minorities. Lithuania is considered relatively safe. However, violent and nonviolent crimes affecting foreigners have occurred throughout the country. Common crimes against foreigners include pickpocketing, thefts, and thefts from cars as well as car thefts.

Telephone connections are generally good, with local Internet cafes offering computer access and ATMs being widely available. Major credit cards are widely accepted.

The medical care standard in Lithuania has improved significantly. However, many medical facilities do not meet Western standards. Only a few private clinics offer medical services nearly equal to Western European or US standards. Most of the basic medical supplies like disposable needles, anesthetics, antibiotics, and other pharmaceuticals are now widely available, but most hospitals and clinics still suffer from a lack of equipment and resources. Serious medical problems requiring hospitalization and/or medical evacuation can cost thousands of dollars or more. This is a problem since doctors and hospitals often expect immediate cash payment for health services.

Tick-borne encephalitis and Lyme disease are common illnesses in Lithuania. In rural areas rabies has been an issue. Another area of health concern is sexually transmitted diseases, which have become a serious public health problem.

Lithuanian streets are above-average in quality, close to those in the United States; however, road conditions can vary quite a bit, ranging from well-maintained two- to four-lane highways connecting major cities, to small dirt roads traversing the countryside. Traffic rules are frequently not obeyed. Traffic laws can be very different from what foreigners are used to; for example, when involved in a traffic accident, moving the car before the police arrive can result in you being charged with hit and run.

Public transportation is considered safe; however, when traveling, personal security awareness should be maintained.

The climate of Lithuania is a typical European continental–influenced climate with warm, dry summers and cold winters. Winter months can be quite cold; January is the coldest month with daytime temperatures usually below the freezing point. Heavy snowfall or even snowstorms are possible during the winter months. During the winter, most major roads are cleared of snow. Year-round the weather is often breezy and humid due to the proximity of the Baltic Sea. During the summer, daytime temperatures average 20°–25°C (68°–77°F) but can go up to 30°C (86°F) or more.

Risk Factors					
Society	Political	Economy	Crime	Environment	Infrastructure
●			●		●

Malaysia

GDP est. (Official Exchange): $303.5 billion (2012 est.)
Capital: Kuala Lumpur
Area (total): 329,847 sq km
Slightly larger than New Mexico
Data from *CIA World Fact Book* (https://www.cia.gov/library/
  publications/the-world-factbook/)

Malaysia used to be known for its raw material exports in the 1970s. Since then the country has transformed itself into one of the top 10 outsourcing locations. In 2003 the Malaysian government started investing in pharmaceuticals, medical technology, and high-technology industries, adding to its existing value-added production chain. In June 2010, the government introduced the Tenth Malaysia Plan, which aims to attract more direct foreign investment. Malaysia is a constitutional monarchy that has an elected federal parliamentary government. Malaysia is considered a multiethnic country of 29.6 million people (July 2013 est.), with Malays forming the predominant ethnic group. The two other large ethnic groups are Chinese and Indians. Islam is the official religion and is practiced by approximately two-thirds of the population. The official language in Malaysia is Bahasa. However, English is widely spoken. During the late-eighteenth and nineteenth centuries, Malaysia was occupied by Britain, and later during World War II it was occupied by Japan.

The cost of living as a percentage to total net income for a person is approximately 27 percent lower than the cost of living in the Philippines or India. Malaysia has its own Silicon Valley known as the Multimedia Super Corridor, which in 2011 had a workforce of around 40,000 outsourcing personnel. Even though the Malaysian government has put various initiatives in the education space into action, the literacy rate of 91 percent is still trailing behind the 93 percent of China and the Philippines.

Malaysia's infrastructure quality is among the highest in the world, with both road quality and electric supply being very comparable to the United States for roads and to Thailand for electric supply.

In 2012 Malaysia was ranked #54 on Transparency International's corruption list. In comparison, the United States was ranked #19 and Germany #13.

Intellectual property protection in Malaysia is higher than in many of its competing outsourcing countries. On the other hand, software piracy is much higher than in the United States

When traveling to the eastern Malaysian states of Sabah and Sarawak (on the island of Borneo) from peninsular Malaysia, or between the provinces of Sabah and Sarawak, foreigners are required to show a passport to the immigration authorities of the respective local state, which have their own immigration authorities, who determine whether you can enter and for how long you can stay.

There remain concerns about the possibility of terrorist attacks against Westerners in Southeast Asia. Some extremist groups in the region have demonstrated the capability to carry out attacks in locations where Westerners congregate. Two groups that have shown anti-Westerner tendencies are Jemaah Islamiyah (JI) and the Abu Sayyaf Group (ASG). At least JI is linked to al-Qaeda, using regional terrorist groups and cells for its operation throughout Southeast Asia.

Kidnapping of Westerners has occurred on the eastern islands and coastal regions of the state of Sabah, perpetrated by criminal and terrorist groups.

Small-scale public demonstrations are occurring more frequently in Kuala Lumpur and environs, sometimes arranged on short notice via social media. Most of those gatherings are peaceful; however some can create violence.

Petty theft, particularly purse snatching and pickpocketing, and residential burglaries are common. Also credit card fraud and automobile theft are common. Lately some thieves carrying knives have slashed and cut victims to shock them into immediately releasing valuable items.

One of the more common methods for credit card fraud is for retailers to swipe the credit card under the counter where a machine transmits the card's information to a criminal organization for reproduction. Some sophisticated criminal organizations have tapped into data lines emanating from retail establishments, allowing credit card information to be stolen while it is being transmitted to a financial institution.

Medical facilities and services are adequate in the larger cities, where Western-trained doctors are available. Travelers who are staying in Malaysia for a longer time should investigate private ambulance services.

The air quality in Malaysia is at acceptable levels most of the year. However, when Malaysia and neighboring countries burn vegetation, especially from March through June and during September and October, the air quality can range from "unhealthy for sensitive groups" to "unhealthy."

It is not uncommon that drivers weave in and out of traffic and run through red lights. This poses a hazard for both drivers and pedestrians unfamiliar with such traffic patterns. The traffic is typically heavy during the morning and afternoon rush hours and slows down considerably when it rains, particularly during the monsoonal rains, which can quickly flood roads located in low-lying areas. Traffic jams are common in major cities because infrastructure development has not kept pace with the proliferation of motorized vehicles. Multilane highways often merge into narrow two-lane roads in the center of town and create more congestion. There have been fatal and other serious accidents involving long-distance tour buses in Malaysia, particularly at night or in adverse weather conditions. If you plan to travel by bus, choose a reputable company and avoid overnight routes. Reports of late-night road rage incidents are common, especially after midnight.

The climate of Malaysia is hot and humid tropical, with all months above 18°C (64.4°F). Depending on the season, the amount of rain can be very drastic. This is typical for tropical climates with a monsoon season. The relative humidity is quite high and ranges between 70 and 90 percent. The temperatures stay around 23°–28°C (73.4°–82.4°F) year round, depending on the area. From July to mid-November, Malaysia can be hit by typhoons, causing heavy damage, flooding, and erosion.

Risk Factors					
Society	Political	Economy	Crime	Environment	Infrastructure
		●	●	●	

Outsourcing Personnel

The cost for personnel has driven most outsourcing companies to recruit more and more in low-cost countries. Some outsourcing companies have gone to such an extreme extent that even personnel from traditional low-cost countries such as India and the Philippines are augmented with personnel from even lower cost countries such as Egypt. The resources in those countries, which are even cheaper, usually provide internal services to personnel in the outsourcing company, like an internal help desk. Some groups of personnel are typical of outsourcing companies. In this section we are going to take a look at these various groups. Please keep the following quote in mind, when reading the next paragraphs. It is from Sun Tzu's famous book *The Art of War**: "If you know the enemy and know yourself, you need not fear the result of a hundred battles. If you know yourself but not the enemy, for every victory gained you will also suffer a defeat. If you know neither the enemy nor yourself, you will succumb in every battle." Please take his words with a grain of salt. Outsourcing personnel are not your enemies. Even though sometimes it will feel like they are, this is when you should remember what you have read here.

Consulting Personnel

A number of outsourcing organizations are consulting companies. Some of them were always organizations with mixed businesses. Others were just consulting organizations that at some point decided to go the direction of outsourcing. The reason for many of those companies is the traditionally "very spiky" consulting business and the stable revenue stream from multiyear outsourcing deals allow for a more steady revenue stream and better personnel planning. One of the main advantages those former consulting companies bring to the table is experienced consultants. Some of those consulting companies move consultants that are no longer progressing in their career into their outsourcing practice. According to some recent developments, the outsourcing industry might have to reshape and offer cutting-edge people. This could position the outsourcing companies with consulting

---

* Sun Tzu. 2009. *The Art of War*. L. Giles, B. Williams, and Sian Kim, translators. Shawn Connors, ed. El Paso, TX: El Paso Norte Press, Special Edition Books.

practices in a better position in the market than the companies that are doing only outsourcing.

Former Employees of Clients

A large number of outsourcing organizations will "rebadge" employees from clients and make them employees of the outsourcing company. They continue their work, having the same job as before. Sometimes they earn the same amount of money, and sometimes less. Sometimes they perform their previous job functions only to have an individual with a lower salary learn and take over their position within months. In this case when they have finished teaching those individuals, they either become part of the outsourcing organization or are laid off. This group of individuals consists mainly of older individuals who have had the same job for a long time and are suddenly challenged with the new requirements coming from their new employer, the outsourcing company: Find the best (cheapest) way to deliver service to your old company.

Internal Resources

Particular consulting organizations that went into outsourcing have reached back to internal resources to also serve their clientele on the outsourcing side. Since those internal resources, such as incident management, are used for the outsourcing companies' internal operation, they can be stretched thin. The services they provide are usually offered with no or little customization. Internal resources are usually remote and do not come on-site.

Third-Party Personnel

It is not unusual that outsourcing companies have third parties support them in a deal. Those third parties are sometimes preferred vendors or are already delivering services for the internal organization of the outsourcing company. There are two risks with this setup of the outsourcing company having a preferred vendor:

- When it comes to getting the best service, the choice offered is rather limited, and you might get stuck with a service that you previously might have voted down.
- Outsourcing organizations that are IT resource poor (e.g., they do not own their own data centers) are forced to buy IT services like data center services from a third party. This can create interesting contractual setups. Those outsourcing contracts can usually have more pages than a telephone book of a large city like New York. It is nearly impossible to have such contracts map all requirements across all the parties involved in the outsourcing deal.

Sometimes the business culture between the outsourcing company and the third party supporting them can be the source of disconnects, failures, and friction—particularly when it is the first time the two companies are working together.

Hired Personnel

In most cases, the outsourcing company will hire individuals to provide the outsourcing service to a client. This is sometimes done in a very quick fashion so the outsourcing company is able to deliver the required services in a timely fashion. Those individuals who are new to the outsourcing company are expected to pick up things quickly and those individuals are not always the perfect matches for the open positions. The outsourcing companies that deliver via an onshore delivery model usually place the operation in rural low-cost areas, which are traditionally talent poor. To get the right people, they need to either have people relocate or set the bar very low, allowing less-qualified individuals to be hired. With outsourcing companies that deliver offshore, there is a comparable situation, which is slightly different. Most large outsourcing companies deliver out of large cities (e.g., Bangalore in India), which have a large and skilled resource pool. However, the sheer number of outsourcing companies that are present in such cities allows the skilled individuals to move from company to company, building a resume with well recognizable names of large outsourcing companies on it. This has been known to create huge staff turnover and knowledge exfiltration out of organizations. An engagement might have just reached a point where it starts jiving when key resources decide to move on. The attrition rate in India has been much higher than what we have seen in countries like the United States. *Forbes*[*] magazine, in an article from 2012, mentioned rates of 20–30 percent as normal with up to 50 percent in industries such as IT.

Teams

During an outsourcing engagement you will have usually two teams that you are dealing with, one being the transition team, which is temporarily assigned to your outsourcing engagement. This team will transition out as soon as the run team is up to speed or when the funds for the transition are gone and the run team needs to take on part of the remaining transition activities. Unfortunately, the situation of funds running out seems to happen more often than what someone would wish for.

Transition Team   Many outsourcing companies have a core group of specialists that help set up an engagement and transition services and hardware over to the outsourcing company. The individuals in such transition teams go from client to client, transitioning services to the outsourcing company. This type of work can burn out individuals over time and does not necessary foster creativity in solution engineering. Often, consultants support the transition team by taking on the more challenging jobs or the project management.

Runtime Team   The runtime team, if dedicated, usually consists of individuals newly hired or of third-party personnel that come from a subcontractor of the outsourcing company. Additionally, services are provided by internal resources of the outsourcing company (e.g., incident response), which are shared across clients and the internal operation of the outsourcing company. The runtime team is usually supplemented by former employees of the client who got rebadged—a term that is commonly used in the outsourcing industry, meaning that the individuals do the same work as before but now have an employee

---

[*] http://www.forbes.com/sites/sylviavorhausersmith/2012/07/02/how-to-stop-employee-turnover-in-india/.

badge of the outsourcing company. These employees are usually phased out over time, once the knowledge has been transferred to the runtime team.

Issues with Global Delivery Teams   By now you probably have noticed that the various groups within the team that transitions your service or is scheduled to run it during the outsourcing period are a mix of individuals with various backgrounds, skills, and cultural backgrounds working for the outsourcing company not only directly but also in subcontracting relationships. Anybody who has managed large teams knows that there are more than just "technical" challenges when it comes to forming a team. With large global outsourcing engagements, one aspect becomes even more important—the different cultures of the individuals who make up the team. Issues can arise just from simple miscommunication. The cultural differences are usually an underestimated aspect in a global delivery model. Dutch researcher Geert Hofstede[*] has developed a well-known cultural personality scheme that focuses on the ways in which culture impacts an organization. In his research he defines five dimensions:

1. *Power distance*—The dimension that describes how different parts of a society perceive the differences and inequalities in the society. Some cultures can see everyone as equal in value, even when there are clear differences in wealth, power, education, etc. And in other cultures everyone is very aware of the differences in society, resulting in dissatisfaction or class warfare. High power distance can also be rooted in violent politics and large income inequality.

   The United States is an example of a culture with a large power distance. Incomes can vary quite a bit (1 percent of the population earning the majority of the money versus the 99 percent of the population making significantly less). This situation of income inequality results in many dissatisfied people in the United States. Other regions like Latin America, Asia, and Africa have high power distances, and Germanic countries have usually smaller distances.

---

[*] The Hofstede Centre. http://geert-hofstede.com/countries.html

2. *Individualism vs. collectivism*—Hofstede determined that there are societies that have a strong feeling for individualism, loosely coupling those individuals and requiring each of them to look after themselves. On the other hand there are the collectivist societies that from birth integrate individuals into a group or family, which protects the individual in exchange for unquestioning loyalty.

   The United States is considered a highly individualistic society, as are most of the Western countries. On the other hand, less-developed countries and most Asian countries are considered collectivistic. A special case is Japan, which is considered to fall somewhere in the middle. India with its caste system is an example of a society that integrates an individual from birth into a certain group in the society.

3. *Masculinity vs. femininity*—The naming of this dimension might be misleading. This dimension describes which attributes of each gender are predominant. Male attributes like assertiveness and competitiveness or even aggressiveness are valued higher in some societies than modesty, peacefulness, nurturance, or caring for each other, which are typical female attributes. So this dimension is more about, for example, assertiveness vs. nurturing.

   The United States, Japan, and German-speaking countries are considered masculine societies. On the other side there are the Scandinavian countries and Holland, which are considered more feminine societies. Most Asian (with the exception of Japan) countries and those in Latin America are considered moderately feminine.

4. *Uncertainty avoidance vs. tolerance for uncertainty*—Uncertainty and ambiguity are perceived either as painful and to be avoided or as tolerable and sometimes even pleasurable. These differences go along with strict laws and rules in societies that try to avoid uncertainty. Another attribute of such cultures is that individuals tend to be more emotional and nervous about the future. On the other hand, in some societies individuals are more tolerant of different opinions and have fewer rules, enjoying the differences of opinions. In these societies individuals tend to not express their emotions openly.

The United States is to a large part moderately tolerant of uncertainty; however, many groups within the United States clearly are not. German-speaking countries, Japan, and countries in Latin America are usually higher in uncertainty avoidance than English-speaking countries, Scandinavian countries, and Chinese-speaking countries, which are lower in uncertainty avoidance. This dimension has a direct influence on the business cultures in those countries.

5. *Long-term vs. short-term orientation*—This dimension reflects on gratification and how a culture approaches it. In societies with long-term orientation, values like perseverance and thrift are important. In societies that are short-term oriented, the value of tradition, social obligations, and protecting "face" are much more important.

Long-term orientation can be found in East Asian countries, especially Chinese-speaking countries, Japan, and Korea. This long-term orientation seems to be tied to national growth and the citizens' emphasis on thrift and perseverance!

In a global delivery model the five personality dimensions add to/magnify the normal friction that stems from having personnel with different personality traits on the team. Based on how individuals perceive their co-workers, their work, their relationship to the outsourcing company and the world in general, conflict is just a question of time.

Salaries

Outsourcing companies are not known for high salaries. Personnel working for an outsourcing company are usually paid at the lower end of the salary range where an individual with a particular skill set would be found. This is not necessarily true for hot markets like India, where outsourcing companies are still experiencing a shortage of talent with specific skills. In recent years the competition has cooled down a little due to the overwhelming number of graduates that Indian universities have produced; however, some skills are still in high demand.

Growth Strategies

When dealing with an outsourcing company, you will find two types: ones that grew organically (i.e., success allowed the business to grow) and others that grew by acquisitions. There is probably not one outsourcing organization that has done only one or the other. However, some organizations are on one side or the other side of the spectrum. The organizations that grew mainly organically usually show a strong culture, and the overall governance seems to be more mature, resulting in functioning security processes and frameworks that allow for the replication of solutions. On the other side, there are the organizations that mainly grew by acquisitions and/or mergers. The merger and acquisition growth strategy in theory allows for faster growth of delivery capabilities. In reality, mergers and acquisitions are one of the leading reasons why organizations fail and eventually fold, according to an article[*] published by *Harvard Business Review* in 2008. The general misperception that drives growth by acquisition is, "The whole is always greater than the sum of its parts." Cultural differences, and particularly the forming of tribes,[†] where tribe members would rather deal with another tribe member than the best "wo-man for the job," results most of the time in less than what the two parts made up individually. The urge to form tribes usually is found in middle management, particularly with organizations that are small to midsize and have not reached a maturity level that requires the establishment of solid governance, which would not allow for tribal thinking. It is advisable to research the history of an outsourcing company to avoid any surprises later on. Subpar performance on the outsourcing company side can have serious negative impact on your compliance and security. Usually activities related to security and compliance are perceived as overhead and prime candidates to be cut, that is, not executed, just to save time and money.

---

[*] http://hbr.org/2008/09/seven-ways-to-fail-big/ar/pr
[†] http://www.evancarmichael.com/Women-Entrepreneurs/4531/Rising-Above-the-Tribal-Nature-for-Success-in-Business.html

2

THE CLOUD

Nowadays the term *cloud* is probably one of the most overused terms in the IT industry. For the purpose of this book the definition given by the National Institute of Standards and Technology (NIST) as published in March 2011 is used. Figure 2.1 shows on a high level how NIST sees the current cloud offerings in the market. However, there already are "flavors" of cloud services that NIST does not really address. We will take a closer look at some of them later in this chapter in "Beyond the Cloud."

Some people have problems in understanding what exactly the various cloud definitions mean. The following sections will provide you with a definition for the three service models and the three deployment models. Any combination of service model and deployment model is theoretically possible. Some might not make much sense for most organizations; however, they might be a fit for others.

Software as a Service (SaaS)

The capability provided to the consumer is to use the provider's applications running on a cloud infrastructure. The applications are accessible from various client devices through a thin client interface such as a web browser (e.g., web-based e-mail). The consumer does not manage or control the underlying cloud infrastructure including network, servers, operating systems, storage, or even individual

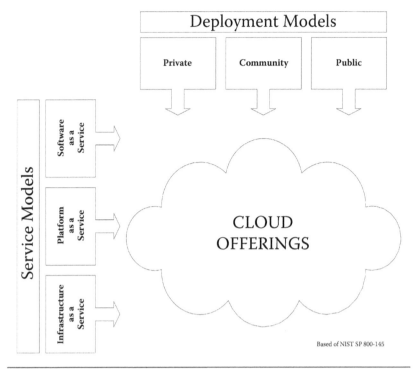

Figure 2.1   Cloud offerings.

application capabilities, with the possible exception of limited user-specific application configuration settings.[*]

Platform as a Service (PaaS)

The capability provided to the consumer is to deploy onto the cloud infrastructure consumer-created or acquired applications created using programming languages and tools supported by the provider. The consumer does not manage or control the underlying cloud infra-structure including network, servers, operating systems, or storage,

---

[*] Source: NIST SP 800-145 (Draft, January 2011).

but has control over the deployed applications and possibly application hosting environment configurations.[*]

Infrastructure as a Service (IaaS)

The capability provided to the consumer is to provision processing, storage, networks, and other fundamental computing resources where the consumer is able to deploy and run arbitrary software, which includes operating systems and applications. The consumer does not manage or control the underlying cloud infrastructure but has control over operating systems, storage, deployed applications, and possibly limited control of select networking components (e.g., host firewalls).[†]

Private Cloud

In general private clouds are operated solely for a single organization (Figure 2.2). They can be hosted and managed internally or by a third party. Going with a private cloud in-house is for some companies more of a technology decision and for others a business decision. There is no general rule why organizations go the route of a private cloud. If a private cloud is deployed in-house there are some factors to consider:

- **Up-front investment**—To build your own private cloud, you will have to invest in hardware and, depending on what cloud framework you want to use, also in software and training for the IT personnel to build and maintain the private cloud.
- **Scalability limits (in-house)**—To achieve cost savings, your organization is very likely to limit the physical cloud servers to a number that your organization deems necessary to provide service during the maximum demand expected. This

---

[*] Source: NIST SP 800-145 (Draft, January 2011).
[†] Source: NIST SP 800-145 (September 2011).

Private Cloud

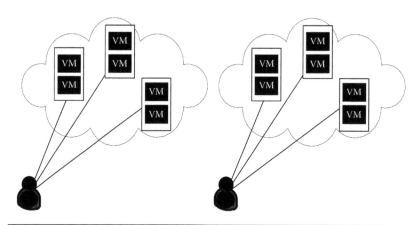

Figure 2.2 Private cloud.

addresses scalability requirements but limits the elasticity of the cloud environment.

- **Total control over security (in-house)**—A private cloud that is maintained by your IT personnel provides you with total control over its security. On the other hand a private cloud maintained or hosted by a third party offers better security than a community or public cloud hosted by a third party.

Community Cloud

A community cloud is operated for a group of organizations sharing an "interest," such as compliance/security with a specific standard (Figure 2.3). Community clouds can be seen as public clouds that are limited to a group of tenants. However, many of the security concerns that are applicable to the public cloud are also applicable to a community cloud, due to the shared usage model.

Public Cloud

The cloud model that has been debated the most is the public cloud, and it is probably being used by most organizations that have decided to use the cloud for the delivery of some or potentially all of their IT

Community Cloud

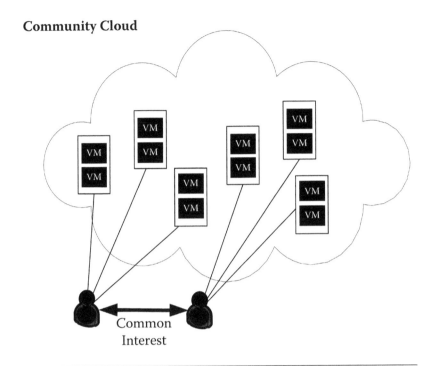

Figure 2.3　Community cloud.

services (Figure 2.4). Particular storage in the public cloud has taken off (e.g., Dropbox, Google Drive, Microsoft Drive). Public cloud services are made available to the general public or a large industry group and are usually owned by an organization selling cloud services. Examples of public cloud services are Amazon's Elastic Compute Cloud (EC2), Microsoft's Azure Services Platform, IBM's Blue Cloud, Sun Cloud, or Google AppEngine. The reason why this deployment model has taken off becomes clear when looking at some of the key benefits:

- **No initial investment**—Hardware and network are both provided by the cloud service provider.
- **Highly scalable**—Additional servers can usually be available within seconds or hours, compared with weeks or months when having to order hardware.
- **Elasticity**—In case of unforeseen demand for service, the elasticity of the public cloud can address this short-term demand by additional virtual instances.

Public Cloud

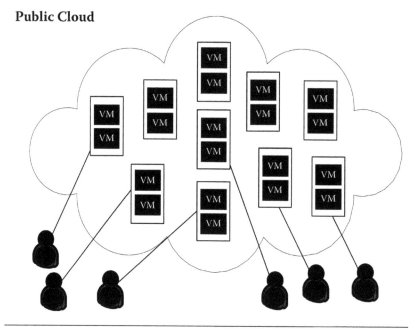

Figure 2.4   Public cloud.

- **Pay for what you use**—In the public cloud, you pay only for resources that you use.

The public cloud has also some disadvantages that you need to be aware of. Not all public cloud service providers support all platforms. Some exotic computing platforms are not supported at all.

Hybrid Clouds

A hybrid cloud (Figure 2.5) is a combination of two standard deployment models as identified by NIST (private, community, or public). Hybrid clouds offer the benefits (and some of the disadvantages) of each of the deployment models. A hybrid cloud deployment could allow an organization to use public cloud computing resources to meet temporary needs and use a private cloud for everyday computing needs. The capability of using cloud resources that come from a different deployment model is called *cloud bursting*, allowing for scaling across clouds. A primary advantage of cloud bursting is that an organization pays only for extra computing resources when they are

Hybrid Cloud

Private cloud bursting into
Public cloud

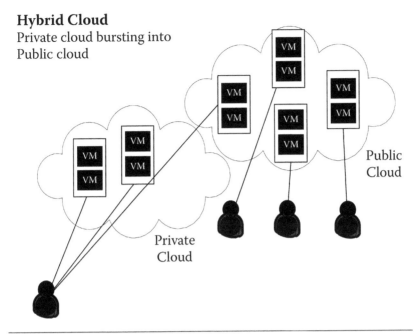

Public
Cloud

Private
Cloud

Figure 2.5 Hybrid cloud.

needed. Security is usually a major concern when it comes to cloud bursting since it is not guaranteed that the cloud that provides the additional resources has the same level of security or is even hosted in the same geographic location (some cloud service providers—but not all—guarantee a certain geographic location).

What the Cloud Is and Is Not

Listening to some cloud enthusiasts, you could think that the cloud is the silver bullet that addresses all of our IT problems. Cloud computing is here to stay. Some organizations will find that moving to the cloud does not result in the expected cost savings simply because of the additional security required or the modifications that applications require to take advantage of a cloud environment. All these additional expenses can easily negate any cost savings that a cloud environment would offer. In other cases the level of security might not be appropriate for the data that the application handles, even though more and more organizations lower their risk acceptance level. Another factor for not adopting the cloud might be the outages that seem to be common and have resulted in service disruptions with big name companies. The verbiage that one major cloud provider added to his Service Level Agreement (SLA), clearly stating that outages of the cloud services of less than a certain number of minutes do not count against the promised SLA, might not encourage organizations with uptime-sensitive applications to move them to that particular cloud service provider (CSP). So what exactly is the problem with the above SLA statement? It basically means that a CSP could experience an outage of two minutes, have service come back for one minute and then become unavailable for another two minutes, and still consider this as 100 percent availability/uptime (assuming the SLA states three minutes as the limit for an outage). The SLAs of many larger CSPs have become the size of a telephone book, allowing the CSP to get away with situations that would be unheard of in a traditional hosting contract.

Beyond the Cloud

Cloud computing has become a part of the modern IT landscape. Organizations are implementing cloud solutions mainly for cost savings; however, cloud computing is beyond cost savings, allowing organizations to address resource issues that were impossible to solve in the past. The typical characteristics[*] of cloud computing are as follows:

- **On-demand self-service**—A consumer can unilaterally provision computing capabilities.
- **Broad network access**—Capabilities are available over the network.
- **Resource pooling**—The provider's computing resources are pooled to serve multiple consumers using a multitenant model, with different physical and virtual resources dynamically assigned and reassigned according to consumer demand.
- **Rapid elasticity**—Capabilities can be rapidly and elastically provisioned, in some cases automatically, to quickly scale out, and rapidly released to quickly scale in.

---

[*] Source: NIST SP 800-145.

- **Measured service**—Cloud systems automatically control and optimize resource use by leveraging a metering capability at some level of abstraction appropriate to the type of service.

So why are security and privacy in the cloud a concern? Traditional safeguards that security experts have been familiar with for decades have been removed. New ways of achieving the same level of security have yet to be developed. However, since cloud security is so new, it is not well understood in the sense of risks and countermeasures. Right now the cloud security model is heavily relying on the hypervisor (the software that brokers between the hardware and the various operating systems) forming a barrier that separates the various virtual machines from each other. If someone discovers a flaw in the hypervisor that ultimately allows circumventing or crashing the hypervisor, then this will have a significant impact on the public cloud model, that allows multiple tenants to be on the same hardware platform. What would happen if a hacker group buys virtual server in a public cloud, just to disrupt service or steal your valuable business information? There are some other factors that make security experts nervous, particularly with the public cloud model:

- According to NIST, "There is a sense of location independence in that the consumer generally has no control or knowledge over the exact location of the provided resources but may be able to specify location at a higher level of abstraction (e.g., country, state, or datacenter)" (SP 800-145).
- The cloud infrastructure is made available to the general public or a large industry group and is owned by an organization *selling* cloud services.

The second bullet point by itself might not be a problem; however, when someone sells something, a service or product, economic principles apply: they need to make a profit or at least a living. Having said that, you can imagine that cloud providers are trying to shave off any expense they can, just to stay competitive. The number of public cloud providers seems to already have climbed into the hundreds, with no end to the growth anytime soon.

Virtual Private Cloud

The cloud industry probably has not slept one night since the first marketing person coined the name *cloud*. Cloud is nothing new; it is a combination of technologies that have been around for awhile, with the main technologies being used for virtualization in combination with rapid provisioning and deprovisioning. The virtualization makes up the core of cloud services. Nowadays, there are various "flavors" that go beyond the general types of cloud services: IaaS, PaaS, or SaaS. Virtual private cloud (VPC) is just one of these flavors, allowing the customers to use their internal resources (e.g., database) instead of the cloud provider services. In most cases the cloud provider is not going to virtualize your heavyweight IT systems (e.g., large database servers). What that means is that any application that you put in the public cloud will be required to use the cloud provider's shared database server (that this is a shared database by itself can already make some security professionals shiver). If this is not the same brand that you had before, you will need to adapt your application to it, so it can use the CSP's database server. In a VPC you have virtual private networks that are established between the cloud and your IT environment, allowing you to keep the database server in-house and still put the application into the cloud. There are other flavors that cloud providers have come up with, to distinguish themselves from the crowd of CSPs, with hundreds of companies playing in the cloud service space.

Standardization between CSPs

It seems that each cloud provider uses its own proprietary approach to "glue" the cloud components together. This requires cloud consumers to buy into this glue, customizing their solution to the proprietary layer that the cloud provider keeps to himself. The lack of standardization continues with the number of solutions that have been developed to ensure that customer data stays confidential. One of the biggest disadvantages, taking a conservative stand, is the fact that cloud solutions are monocultures. One of the characteristics, the elasticity of a cloud, can only be achieved by standardization. Large numbers of the same hardware, operating system (OS), software, network device, and so forth are being used. Some outages have been traced back to vendor updates that were buggy and affected all of the upgraded devices in the cloud, a giant that got sick due to a microbe. If a buggy update is deployed, it can cause major outages of the cloud environment.

Compliance in the Cloud

Another aspect is the compliance requirements in the cloud. Many outsourcing companies offering cloud services advertise their cloud services as being, for example, compliant with the Payment Card Industry Data Security Standards (PCI DSS). This might sound tempting to some companies that have struggled with a cost-efficient way to achieve PCI DSS compliance; however, what the cloud offers is an infrastructure that has been certified to a certain standard with *no* customer applications included (i.e., no applications run in the cloud). A certified infrastructure does not mean that the whole solution is still certified after the application and data have been deployed and loaded into the cloud. Even if you have an application that is certified in your current environment (i.e., infrastructure), it might no longer be certified in the cloud. The equation of application (certified before deployment) + infrastructure (certified before deployment) does not always work out to the sum of both being certified.

Security and Privacy Issues with Cloud Computing

Everyone is talking about cloud computing being insecure and that it puts at risk information and applications that are running in a cloud environment. Let's take a closer look at what the cloud offers in regard to confidentiality, integrity, and availability.

Scalability versus Elasticity

For many organizations the availability of their services is important. In traditional IT environments, that meant that you had to invest in the hardware and software that could handle peak demand of a service or application that you offered to your customers. In cloud environments this is no longer valid. A peak in demand for your service that is maybe a once in a year situation no longer requires the infrastructure be scaled to that one time event. You can take advantage of the elasticity of the cloud, which provisions new servers and applications as the demand for your service increases. Once the demand goes down, the additional servers and applications are removed, and you no longer pay for them. On the other hand, your business (hopefully) grows or shrinks, and you will require more or fewer cloud resources to address the basic demand that you see over the majority of the year. This is where scalability comes into the picture. In general you can say that spiky businesses (e.g., Victoria's Secret with their on-line shows, Federal Student Financial Aid with twice a year deadlines, or the IRS with its April 15th deadline) have to worry more about elasticity than the typical organization that uses the cloud for internal operation with a relatively stable head count.

On-Demand Self-Service

With on-demand self-service, cloud environments differentiate themselves from traditional IT environments. The CSP has virtual images of hosts that make up your cloud environment. Those images are stored either centralized or separated by cloud tenants. A centralized storage results in a shared environment that all cloud tenants use to store their images. As always, when sharing resources, the opportunity for the bad guys to break into another account is there. CSPs advertise with verbiage like, "XYZ provides a simple *web-based portal* that allows full control over your virtual machines. Upload virtual appliances or virtual machines directly, and then configure IP and network settings with ease." Even with an actual separation of the storage by tenant, the web front-end offered by the cloud provider is very likely the same for all cloud tenants, introducing the same risks as any other web application that is accessible over the Internet. One difference is that with this web application you provide access to all server (virtual host images) that make up your cloud environment. This type of attack is applicable to all forms of cloud that are hosted by a public CSP.

Rapid Elasticity

This attribute allows for (theoretically) unlimited resources to address any demand for resources. As always in life, this advantage comes with a price tag—not only in the form of money that goes to the CSP, but also in the form of increased risk. Elasticity is achieved by cloning resources and load balancing between all resources of the same type in the cloud. This cloning unfortunately results in a loss of integrity with your logs. At a cloud resource level, the cloning is visible, but at an application level, the cloning might not be visible. For example, instead of one web server, suddenly two web servers are logging into a central log server. (Note: Local logging in a cloud environment does not make much sense due to the fact that an instance of a server can be decommissioned at any given time, resulting in the loss of all local data.) At any given time the second web server can be decommissioned, stopping the logging to the centralized log server. Looking at the log file might show a problem with one of the web servers; however, in the worst case scenario, one could not distinguish between the two servers, or the server that logged the problem may no longer be available.

Here is another example that should further clarify the problem of cloud elasticity: imagine a group of users that shares the same login credentials. In most cloud setups, clones of the same system use the same login credentials to log into a database for example. This could result in quite some confusion when a forensic analysis is required on the logins.

Moving or cloning virtual machines from one physical server to another, such as when you employ dynamic resource scheduling (DRS) or Microsoft's performance and resource optimization (PRO), the network monitoring systems might pick up those new virtual machines, generating alarms that are false positives. Either your network intrusion detection system is very loosely configured to not trigger, or it is very tightly configured and you have to deal with many false positive alerts.

Resource Pooling

Another area of concern in a public cloud environment is resource allocation or, to be more precise, the availability of your applications in the cloud. A Distributed Denial of Service (DDoS) attack against one tenant of a public or semipublic cloud could result in all cloud tenants' applications being impacted.

Outages

First praised as the silver bullet for availability, the cloud has lost some of its reputation, with major cloud outages at large CSPs like Amazon, Microsoft, and others. Every major CSP has had at least one outage. Cloud environments are monocultures; if they get "sick," they get *really* sick—meaning a problem with the cloud infrastructure is usually something that replicates, since devices and systems in the cloud are standardized and show the same vulnerability across all systems of the same type.

Denial of Service

Another aspect of availability is how resources are allocated. A flaw in the resource allocation mechanism or a successful attack could result in a denial of service situation. This is true not only for the virtual environment that clones systems but also for services like domain name service (DNS) recursors that are incorrectly configured, allowing for DDoS attacks against even the largest CSPs. This threat became obvious in the spring of 2013 with Spamhaus, a nonprofit organization that advertises spam lists, that are being used by many ISPs to filter out spam e-mails for their users. Your organization does not even need to be the target of the DDoS; however, if one of the other tenants in the cloud is the target, the scalability of the cloud does not help against a network-based DDoS.

Virtualization Security

Virtualization technology has been around for quite some time. Today two main virtualization technologies make up the majority of the solutions available:

- **Type 1—The hypervisor runs directly on the bare hardware**. Guest operating systems run on top of the hypervisor. Examples for Type 1 hypervisors include Microsoft's Hyper-V and VMware's ESX.

- **Type 2—The hypervisor is also called** *hosted hypervisor.* The hypervisor runs as a program in the host OS. Virtual machines run on top of the Type 2 hypervisor. Examples of Type 2 hypervisors include Oracle VirtualBox, Parallels, Virtual PC, VMware Fusion, VMware Server, Xen, and XenServer.

These two types of hypervisors have their individual weaknesses and advantages. In most of the cases you will find Type 1 hypervisor solutions in cloud environments and Type 2 hypervisor solutions in desktop virtualization environments. However, there is no rule about what a CSP needs to use.

Metering

The metering of resources itself is not the problem, but it is another factor in an equation that got more complex when cloud services were introduced to the IT world. These metering mechanisms that determine what you need to pay can be the target of an attack, trying to manipulate the mechanism to believe that you have used extensive cloud resources, which you need to pay for. In a Denial of Service (DoS) attack, the resources being used result in an extensive bill since you pay for use of resources in the cloud. In a traditional IT infrastructure you pay for power, support, rack space, and cooling, where a DoS attack will also result in higher costs but not significantly higher costs. In a metered cloud you might have to pay for additional hosts that the cloud automatically provisions, serving the demand or additional computing cycles or HTTP/GET requests, depending on your cloud model and contract.*

Hypervisor Security

In a virtualized computing environment, we have replaced the borders of hardware with the hypervisor, which brokers the access to the underlying hardware that all virtual machines share on a hardware host. The level of virtualization, removing traditional boundaries to a

---

* http://www.ibm.com/developerworks/cloud/library/cl-cloudmetering/.

level that even the network between two virtual hosts is virtual, has created new security problems.

Virtual Networks

With the introduction of virtual networks and virtual switches, new problems for network security have arisen. The traditional NIDS and Network Intrusion Prevention System (NIPS) cannot see the traffic that flows across the virtual network between the virtual machines. A potential infection due to a worm that replicates across the network is invisible to the NIDS/NIPS that only sees traffic going and coming from the hardware host, not the network traffic that flows between all the virtual machines on that particular hardware host. Some companies have come up with solutions that potentially can help with this situation, providing virtual NIDS/NIPS solutions. Unfortunately, those solutions usually require a virtual instance dedicated to NIDS/NIPS, taking away capacity from the hardware host. This might be one reason why this technology has not gotten the traction that you would expect. A workaround to this is that some CSPs turn off the internal virtual switch, forcing traffic to always go the way of the physical network interface.

Memory Allocation/Wiping

One area of concern for some security experts is the allocation and wiping of memory that virtual machines use. It is a result of the elasticity of the cloud, which happens not only vertically (more machines) but also horizontally (more memory, additional CPU cores). The OS that runs on a virtual machine is responsible for the memory management. If the OS does not properly wipe the memory before it frees it up, then there is the chance that data is left behind in those memory blocks, which another virtual machine then allocates. This is true for disc storage as well as actual RAM. An attacker could in theory just allocate memory and read it before initializing it, to potentially gain access to passwords or other sensitive data that another virtual machine had left behind. To execute this type of attack, an attacker only needs to request new virtual instances or more memory and release it after reading the new memory that had been allocated to the virtual machine. In a very busy public cloud environment, there is a chance that the attacker gains access to some confidential data eventually, even though modern operating systems have gotten much better in addressing such issues, still they are not perfect.* If you have an application that uses confidential data, it is probably a good idea to have the application overwrite the content of a memory block (variable, field, etc.) with a special routine. Solutions like VMware DRS and PRO can help in load balancing across multiple hosts and also in scrubbing any resources, especially storage and RAM, before they are reassigned. When a CSP uses such a solution, this can add an additional layer of security. Just make sure that the CSP uses the memory scrubbing setting and that memory and storage are scrubbed before being reused.

Cloud Network Configuration

One of the key network elements of cloud is Virtual Local Area Networks (VLAN). So what are VLANs, and why are they so important for the cloud? VLANs are the veins that allow data to circulate through the cloud, strictly separated by each tenant of the cloud. VLANs are configured at a switch level, distinguishing network traffic based on one out of the five criteria:

- **VLAN membership by port**—The ports on a switch are assigned a particular VLAN. For example, if a switch has 8 ports, ports 1 to 4 may be configured to belong to VLAN 1, and ports 5 to 8 may be configured with VLAN 2.
- **VLAN membership by MAC address**—The MAC address of the network interface card (NIC) determines what VLAN a switch assigns to the port that the NIC is connected to.
- **Membership by protocol type**—The layer 2 header containing the protocol type field is used by the switch to decide to which VLAN to associate a network packet.
- **Membership by IP subnet address**—The VLAN association is based on the layer 3 header. The switch determines, based on the layer 3 IP address, the association to a VLAN.

---

* http://www.cs.purdue.edu/homes/bb/cs590/papers/secure_vm.pdf

In many modern cloud configurations, switches are able to assign Private VLAN (PVLAN) IDs based on the IP subnet address. Private VLANs are divided into two groups:

- **Primary PVLAN**—Primary PVLANs are divided into smaller groups called secondary PVLANs.
- **Secondary PVLANs**—Secondary PVLANs exist only inside the primary PVLAN they are assigned to. Each secondary PVLAN has a unique VLAN ID associated to it. Each packet traveling through a PVLAN is tagged with the associated ID of the PVLAN, just as a normal VLAN.

Switches that carry PVLAN traffic can be configured to behave in one out of three ways:

- **Promiscuous**—A node (e.g., host) attached to a port in a promiscuous secondary PVLAN may send and receive packets to any network node in any other secondary PVLAN associated to the same primary PVLAN. Typically routers are attached to promiscuous ports.
- **Isolated**—A node attached to a port in an isolated secondary PVLAN may only send to and receive packets from the promiscuous PVLAN. Typically physical hosts carrying virtual machines (VMs) are connected to isolated ports.
- **Community**—A node attached to a port in a community secondary PVLAN may send to and receive packets from other ports in the same secondary PVLAN, as well as send to and receive packets from the promiscuous PVLAN.

Depending on the type of port configuration, hosts are not able to communicate with each other, even if they belong to the same group (e.g., isolated) (Figure 2.6). This adds an additional layer of security compared with traditional VLANs.

This means that each tenant in a cloud environment has a different subnet that belongs to the virtual servers of that tenant. The switches route the traffic between virtual hosts based on the VLAN ID assigned to the traveling packets. Depending on the port configuration (promiscuous, isolated, or community) traffic can travel directly between virtual hosts (promiscuous and community) or not (isolated).

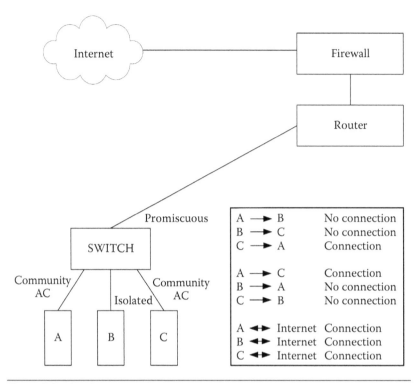

Figure 2.6 PVLAN.

The hypervisor will do its part to map the traffic coming from the physical NIC to the respective virtual NICs of the VM.

This small introduction to VLANs and PVLANs might already give you an idea of how complex cloud network configurations can become (Figure 2.7). Most of this is automated. However the complexity is traditionally the enemy of security. A misconfiguration of the switch fabric could have a disastrous impact on the security in the cloud. Sources for that could be a buggy firmware update for switches or routers with incorrect routing or simply human error (e.g., connecting the wrong devices).

Firewalls in the Cloud

Many CSP's public cloud installations rely on physical load balancers and physical firewalls that segment the cloud environment. One segment is the *demilitarized zone* (connection to the Internet and the back end), and another segment is the *back end zone* (no connection

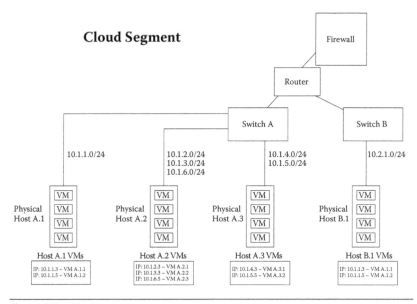

Figure 2.7   Cloud segment.

to the Internet). If there is the need for further segmentation, then this is usually achieved with virtual firewalls. The problem with this approach is that the configuration of the virtual firewalls can be quite tricky, particularly if a solution scheduled to be deployed was not written for a cloud environment. The elasticity of the cloud environment can further add to this complexity. Looking at the virtual firewall approach, with the firewall being implemented at the virtualization layer, you will notice that there is a "software connection" between the virtual machines via the hypervisor that a malicious user could use to connect two virtual machines directly. This is a risk that most cloud users accept. The hypervisor, however, is not the only connection. The virtual switch creates not only a network connection but also a software connection. While drawings show a virtual switch for each virtual machine, in reality most virtualization solutions deploy a single software switch, which is then broken up into multiple logical partitions. This type of configuration is done to minimize the footprint of the switch on the host server. Those are two shortcomings of the virtualization layer that might require a change in the design of the current virtual firewall implementations. Currently there are three types of virtual firewall deployment methods:

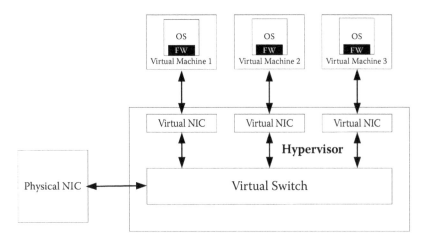

Figure 2.8 Host level firewall.

- **Host level firewalls**—A firewall is installed with each guest OS that runs in a virtual machine (Figure 2.8). In this setup the firewalls are part of the OS image and would be in the category of "personal firewalls" or host level firewalls.
- **Bridge-mode virtual firewalls**—A firewall appliance is installed and interacts with the virtual switch, routing all traffic that flows through the virtual switch also through the virtual firewall appliance (Figure 2.9).

    This setup has the disadvantage that one of the virtual host slots is occupied by the virtual firewall appliance. Also this setup has a significant weakness in the sense that the virtual switch has to route all traffic through the virtual firewall appliance. A misconfiguration, intentionally or unintentionally, could result in none of the traffic being routed through the virtual firewall appliance.
- **Hypervisor-mode virtual firewalls**—The virtual firewall is part of the hypervisor and the virtual switch.

    This solution approach seems to be the most promising solution. The virtual firewall lives at the virtual switch level of each physical host running a hypervisor (Figure 2.10).

Self-Service

You would think that self-service is a good thing, allowing you to address the need for additional computing power. However, you are

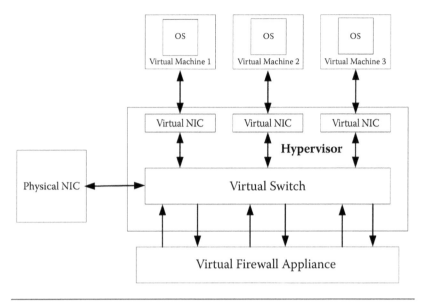

Figure 2.9 Firewall appliance.

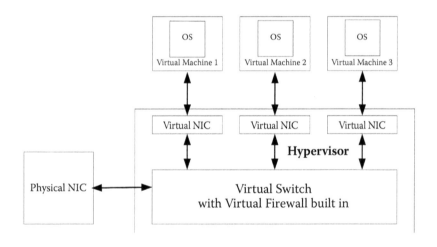

Figure 2.10 Firewall hypervisor.

not the only tenant in a public cloud. There are other cloud tenants that are also happily enjoying the self-service that the CSP offers. In the worst case scenario, all tenants could start spinning up the maximum number of instances in the cloud, all at the same time. This could result in a resource constraint, first with the network and later also with tenants potentially not being able to spin up additional instances of virtual machines.

Malicious Insiders

A well-overlooked area of risk with CSPs is their staff who maintain the cloud environment having access to the hypervisor configuration, the storage, backups, and images that your organization uses in the cloud environment. Someone with malicious intent could easily sabotage the cloud operation or copy images of virtual machines, gaining access to sensitive data that the images contain. Edward Snowden[*] is probably a famous example of a system administrator who used his access to steal information. Depending on the geographic region where the cloud provider hosts its service, the requirements for background investigations will vary quite a bit. The laws that govern your right to data in the cloud or the protection of that data against third-party access can also vary quite a bit across the major outsourcing countries. The initially cheap CSP might become an expensive experience after the data has been stolen, corrupted, or is no longer available. The problem with some of the public cloud offerings is that most CSPs try to avoid providing any geographic boundaries where your data is stored. This can also create serious issues if you have compliance requirements that require you to host the data within a certain geographic region (e.g., European countries).

Availability and Service Level Agreements

Looking at some of the SLAs that CSPs have posted you might start thinking that those provide you with everything you need to ensure availability of your services and data. Let's take a closer look at these SLAs, what to look for, and how to recognize terminology or potential claims that are simply unrealistic and should alert you to the credibility of the CSP. We all like to look our best when we present ourselves. However, some CSPs have come up with claims that, when looked at more closely, have so many exclusions that the perfect case never applies. The nature of technology is that it fails once in a while or needs maintenance, resulting in outages. So those are a given. Whether you have a traditional IT environment or host your applications in the cloud (private or public—it does not matter), SLAs

---

[*] http://www.theguardian.com/world/edward-snowden

can differ from CSP to CSP; but what they all have in common is that an outage will impact your operations in one way or another. At least some of the major players in the CSP market seem to have some commonalty in their SLAs, containing the following sections:

- Definitions—Explaining the definitions used in the SLA
- Claims—Explaining under which circumstances you can get a service credit
- Exclusions—Listing the circumstances or situations when a CSP is not liable for an outage
- Actual SLAs—Those can be two types:
  - Performance characteristics of the service
  - Guaranteed uptime for the cloud service

Let's take a closer look at those sections, starting with the guaranteed uptime. One CSP might offer 99.95 percent as guaranteed uptime and another 99.90 percent. At first this seems not to be a large difference. However, when you do the calculation, a value of 99.95 percent translates into 21 min and 36 sec of downtime each month. On the other hand, an uptime of 99.90 percent translates into 43 min and 12 sec each month. Over the period of a year, your applications are more than double the time not available (8:45:36 compared with 4:22:48) when getting a 99.90 percent uptime guarantee compared with a 99.95 percent uptime guarantee. It is obvious that we all want to have a 100 percent uptime guarantee. However, someone offering this might not be as straightforward to you as you might want him or her to be. CSPs vary in how they express their uptime guarantee.

Some use monthly guarantees; others use annual uptime guarantees. So which one is better? A monthly uptime guarantee seems to be the better deal. Why is that? Monthly uptime guarantees are preferable because the window is smaller, allowing for less time to iron out a potential outage. To better understand this, let's take a look at a scenario: A CSP experiences an outage of 4 h in a particular month and has no further outages for the next 11 months. This would result in an annual uptime of 99.95 percent. However the 4 h outage can have a significant impact on your operations. On the other hand, a monthly uptime guarantee of 99.95 percent would result in a maximum allowable monthly outage time of 21 min and 36 sec. A 4 h outage would in this case entitle you to at least a service credit with a CSP that has a *monthly* uptime guarantee of 99.95 percent, but not with the CSP that uses an *annual* uptime guarantee of 99.95 percent. The devil is in the details. In this case it is the difference between monthly and annual uptime guarantee.

It is important that these uptime promises are made for the cloud as a whole, which brings up another interesting part of the SLA to understand: hardware failures. Hardware failed in traditional data centers, and it is going to fail in cloud environments. It is important to understand that if a server that had your virtual image on it fails, the uptime SLA of the cloud is usually not applied. Hardware failures are traditionally excluded and can be found in the exclusion section of the SLA, since the cloud tenant is responsible to make a service redundant, avoiding downtime due to an individual hardware failure.

Such outages are normally covered by the exclusion clause of the SLA and are the responsibility of the customer. When deploying an application in the cloud, it is a good idea to follow cloud best practices[*] (not only applicable to Amazon's EC2—even though some of the practices reference EC2-only services). One of them is to always make your services redundant to avoid a hardware failure causing you downtime. These cases are covered by the *acceptable downtime metric,* which is calculated for outages that impact the vast majority of services or customers. Surprisingly, most CSPs seem not to define exactly what "vast majority" means, leaving them some flexibility with the requirement to notify customers. If your applications in the cloud are impacted by an outage, do not expect to be notified. In most cases CSPs try to keep a low profile with outages, and only if the outage becomes press material, then you can expect to see a service credit or a notification. In most cases you are the one that has to prove that you are entitled to a credit. As a last warning, expecting that during a free trial any of the uptime guarantees are in place might prove a very wrong assumption. When using a trial or Beta of a cloud service, it is advisable to use it for what it is intended—to try out the service, not to run any critical production applications in the trial or Beta cloud service.

There is an ever-growing market of so-called secondary CSPs, which provide their services on top of the major cloud vendors. This setup creates quite a dependency on the uptime of the actual CSPs.

---

[*] http://jineshvaria.s3.amazonaws.com/public/cloudbestpractices-jvaria.pdf

Most of the time those secondary CSPs don't publish any standard SLAs but negotiate SLAs in the individual contracts on a customer-by-customer basis. This can be an advantage for you; however, as a fair warning, magic does not happen anywhere—not even with these secondary CSPs. Many will help you to design redundancy into your applications that run in the cloud, to avoid the risk of downtime on the primary CSP. However, it is possible that you will wind up with no uptime guarantee at all, depending on the size of the secondary CSP.

Authentication, Authorization, Accounting

Numerous articles by security professionals have pointed out that CSPs are not there yet, with their implementation of authentication, authorization, and accounting (AAA) in the cloud. These three A's stand for the trail of evidence that could be used in forensic cases, proving that a particular user or system gained access. Below are common definitions for what those three principles stand for:

- **Authentication**—The process where an entity's identity is verified, typically by providing evidence that it holds a specific digital identity such as an identifier and the corresponding credential(s). Examples of credentials are passwords, one-time tokens, digital certificates, digital signatures, and phone numbers (calling/called).
- **Authorization**—The permissions that a particular entity has, relative to a given activity on an object. Typically authorization is tied to the initial authentication when logging on to an application or service. However, authorization may also be determined based on a range of other criteria, for example, time-of-day restrictions, physical location restrictions, or restrictions on number of instances of sessions of the same entity or user. Most basic access can be defined by read, write, change, or delete rights to a specific object (e.g., file or data element).
- **Accounting**—The tracking of network resource consumption by users or systems for the purpose of capacity and trend analysis, cost allocation, and billing. The tracking usually includes the recording of events such as authentication

and authorization failures. This auditing data is recorded to verify the correctness of procedures carried out based on accounting data. In the cloud, the accounting function is tightly coupled with the metering of service and the elasticity of the cloud.

In SaaS the importance of AAA is critical to deliver a successful service to customers and also to bill for it. Even in the private cloud the AAA concept is important to achieve the maximum benefits of cloud computing, allowing for dynamic resource allocation, as they are needed. Only with AAA in place can departments be billed based on their usage of the cloud.

The cloud is a self-service world that makes you as the tenant responsible for making sure the right people have the right access to the right resources at the right time. Currently resources and basic access to those resources are provided by the CSA. More and more CSPs offer provisioning workflows, enabling their customers to have the right people gain access to the necessary resources without waiting for manual IT intervention. To achieve this level of automation, it is critical to properly manage authentication, authorization, and accounting. The criticism that organizations like the Cloud Security Alliance (CSA) have brought forward is mainly targeting the implementation of insecure interfaces to software that is used to manage and interact with cloud services. These interfaces so far have not shown the level of security that a well-designed service or application would have, mainly lacking maturity with authentication, access control, and encryption. The request to use multifactor authentication for those services is echoed by other security experts. Usually multifactor authentication comes with increased cost, which is a sensitive topic with CSPs that have invested quite a bit of money in the infrastructure of a cloud service.

Tenant Credibility

Cloud computing represents what high-speed computing was 20 years ago, available to the broad masses. Massive computing power for the masses that is affordable, readily available, and easily accessible. This also can attract criminals who use the cloud for their purposes, cracking encryption schemes that were considered secure just 2 years ago. Security experts and groups like the CSA are asking that CSPs establish checks to ensure that nobody with malicious intentions can use the power of cloud computing—a valid request that might be difficult to fulfill, at least to a level that can ensure in a majority of cases some level of assurance that the computing power of the cloud is only used for valid business needs.

Address the Cloud Security/Privacy Dilemma

The following sections provide some guidance on how to gain some assurance that a cloud environment is secure (i.e., has an acceptable risk level for your organization).

SAS-70, SOC 1, and SOC 2 Audits

Whoever has looked at offerings from CSPs has probably noticed a number of audit report types that the various CSPs offer, all to demonstrate that the cloud services they offer are secure. One of these audit reports is the SAS-70 audit standard, which has been around for more than 20 years. This standard was officially retired back in 2011 and should no longer be used. The problem with the SAS-70 standard is that it was never intended to be used to assess service organizations that offer collocation, managed servers, or cloud-hosting services for delivering of service; it was intended for accuracy of financial statements. A SAS-70 audit only looked at the controls and processes that the data center operator had identified, and whether they were executed as intended. The SAS-70 audit standard did not establish a minimum bar that the data center operator had to achieve, nor did a benchmark hold data center operators accountable. Its successor, the SSAE 16 (or SOC 1) audit standard, is changing this. However, it is still only focused on internal controls for financial reporting. The SOC 2 audit standard evaluates controls at a service organization with regard to security, availability, processing integrity, confidentiality and privacy. We will revisit the topic of audit standards later in the book (see Chapter 4, Understand What Is Offered section, Audit Reports).

Cryptography and the Cloud

If the data in the cloud were encrypted at any given point of time, assuming the key is secured, we would have solved the problem of security and privacy in the public cloud. Homomorphic* cryptography is one of these silver bullets that cryptography experts have been working on for quite some time.

When using an encryption scheme that is fully homomorphic, the cloud applications can perform meaningful computations on the encrypted data. Unfortunately, at the current time, fully homomorphic encryption schemes have quite a long way to go before they can be used in practice. Zvika Brakerski, Craig Gentry, and Vinod Vaikuntanathan in their white paper titled, "Fully Homomorphic Encryption without Bootstrapping," presented a promising approach to homomorphic encryption.† The approach presented by the three researchers is the basis for a software library implementation called HELib,‡ which is available for free on GitHub. However, to use homomorphic encryption, an application would need to be rewritten, a potentially large and costly effort that in most cases is not feasible.

Until homomorphic encryption becomes more integrated into everyday application development, the advice given by Bruce Schneier, a leading cryptography expert, still holds: have an enforceable contract with the CSP. This advice is nothing new and is not only valid for cloud computing. What Bruce was referring to is that CSPs' terms of service include pages of fine print that ensure that the CSP is not liable. For example, public clouds can be operated in various geographic locations, and exactly where your operation is currently located will not be known to you. This is a serious problem for organizations that process or store certain data that cannot leave a geographic region or country. One public cloud provider now even offers cloud storage in return for local storage. This means that you provide local storage on your hard drive to the cloud. In exchange, you get free cloud storage. The cloud provider claims that the storage on the local drives of its customers is encrypted and that the model that is being used ensures that the data in the cloud is always available,

---

* http://www.americanscientist.org/issues/pub/2012/5/alice-and-bob-in-cipherspace
† http://eprint.iacr.org/2011/277.pdf.
‡ https://github.com/shaih/HElib?buffer_share=a6bab&utm_source=buffer.

even in a disaster situation, such as when a hard drive of a user that provides storage to the cloud crashes. This is just one model of crowd sourcing that CSPs are pursuing. However, the problem of not being able to limit the storage or processing of data to a specific geographic location can become a deal breaker.

Even with information that is not regulated, a user of a public cloud solution can still face other legal issues. The laws that are applicable to the hosting provider and the information processed or stored vary by country. There are already huge differences between Europe and the United States. For example, the definition of pornography varies throughout the world, with some countries being more relaxed and others being very restrictive on what can be shown. Having, for example, medical images stored in an Islamic country could potentially result in the prosecution of the service provider. Iran punishes involvement with pornography by stoning the person to death. This would be an extreme case of what can happen; however, it demonstrates that the model of "location independence" is not without flaws.

Encrypting all your data and not storing the encryption keys in the cloud is one approach. However, this model relies on one safeguard, which is the encryption. AES-256 is, in the year 2012, considered a safe crypto algorithm when used with a "strong" key. In 10 years the use of AES-256 might be considered insecure. Technology advances, and computing power becomes cheaper and cheaper every year. At the same time mathematicians continue to research equations and prime factorization that are the foundation of modern cryptography, coming up with new approaches for how to calculate complex encryption problems faster. So it is just a question of time before your only safeguard is more an annoyance than an obstacle to get to the information you are trying to protect.

Encryption Keys and the Cloud

Due to compliance and security reasons, most CSPs, if not all, have so far recommended not to store encryption keys in the cloud. Some new services (e.g., Amazon's CloudHSM) provide clients who need to meet data security compliance requirements with a way to meet those requirements by using a dedicated Hardware Security Module (HSM) offered by the CSP. Until now CSPs (e.g., Amazon) recommended to many clients that had sensitive data, or the encryption keys to it, not to store it in the cloud but in their own on-premise data centers. This made it impossible for many companies to fully migrate their applications to a CSP-operated cloud. With the offering of HSM by the CSP, clients can now take advantage of encryption-enabled services (e.g., database encryption, digital rights management, public key infrastructure, etc.). HSMs are usually offered in conjunction with the VPC cloud model. The HSM appliances are provisioned inside the user's virtual private cloud (VPC) with an IP address the user specifies. Amazon, for example, advertises that its CloudHSM service has HSMs that are "tamper-resistant appliances that are designed to comply with international (Common Criteria EAL4+) and US government (NIST FIPS 140-2) regulatory standards for cryptographic modules."*

However, HSM VPC solutions are not cheap. It shows that this service is intended less for the mainstream market than for the organizations that are heavily regulated and would take a high risk if they could not ensure that encryption keys in a cloud environment are securely stored.

Third-Party Cloud Security Providers

More and more third-party security providers are offering cloud security solutions to address the lack of security and privacy with some CSPs. Today (2013) this is still an immature market and is still developing. It is expected that some of the approaches and technologies that are currently offered by those third-party companies will become part of the standard security and privacy services that CSPs offer. The offerings of these third parties vary in their approaches, in what they can offer with a particular cloud model, or in which CSP is supported. The general problem with the model of having a third party providing security services for the cloud is that the third party is at the mercy of the CSP. Any change that the CSP makes to their service or the API used by the third party can result in significant issues in providing their services to you. This can go so far that the third party is no longer able to provide any service to you.

---

* http://aws.amazon.com/cloudhsm/#highlights

FedRAMP and the Federal Cloud

The US government's Office of Management and Budget (OMB) issued in late 2010 a "Cloud First" policy. This requires the US federal government to first evaluate a cloud-based solution before investigating other solutions. This policy tries to achieve cost savings by using cloud technology, which has lower costs than the traditional IT solutions. As a next step in OMB's efforts to achieve cost savings, the federal government established a federal cloud certification with the Federal Risk and Authorization Management Program (FedRAMP). FedRAMP's cloud certification allows CSPs to demonstrate their compliance with the requirements of the Federal Information Security Management Act (FISMA)* for a moderate rated system. At the current time, FISMA identifies three levels of system categorization: High, Medium, and Low. Those levels have been defined in the Federal Information Processing Standard (FIPS) 199.† The security controls that are implemented with a cloud which has been categorized as moderate and is certified by FedRAMP can be found in NIST SP 800-53,‡ which is constantly revised and updated. It can be said that clouds that have been certified by FedRAMP offer better security than the plain vanilla clouds that CSPs offer to the public. Choosing a CSP that has a FedRAMP-certified cloud offering does not mean that all the work has been done and that all security concerns have been addressed. It just means that the underlying cloud infrastructure has met the NIST SP 800-53 requirements for security controls, which are required for a moderate system according to FISMA. Depending on the sensitivity of your data, this might not be sufficient or might be overkill. In any case, the cloud certification does not take any applications in consideration that might be installed in a cloud environment!

How to Securely Move to the Cloud

There is no general approach on how to move a traditional IT environment into a cloud environment. Today's IT allows for so many different ways to implement a solution that each requires a detailed

---

* http://csrc.nist.gov/groups/SMA/fisma/index.html.
† http://csrc.nist.gov/publications/fips/fips199/FIPS-PUB-199-final.pdf.
‡ http://csrc.nist.gov/publications/PubsSPs.html.

analysis before it can be adopted to take full advantage of a cloud environment. However, the following are general guidelines when it comes to security controls migration:

- A traditional security control is available in the cloud and can be used to map/transition the control into the cloud. The control can stay in place and very likely requires only some configuration changes.
- A traditional security control's objective maps to the same objective of a security control in the cloud. The cloud security control is different from the traditional security control. The cloud security control would replace the traditional control in the cloud.
- The traditional security control cannot be used in a cloud environment, and no cloud security control exists that has the same control objective. In this case an analysis needs to be performed to see which compensating controls are available in the cloud that would result in an acceptable residual risk level.
- Identify controls that address cloud-specific risks that are introduced by running an application or storing information in a cloud environment.

The most challenging task is to understand the game changers that the cloud introduced. For example, cloud elasticity: an IP address does not mean much in the cloud. It is assigned at one point in time to a virtual instance of a host. The moment the instance is not needed anymore, the cloud decommissions the virtual host, releasing the IP, which then can be reused with another virtual instance of another host, which might belong to another tenant of the cloud. Host-level authenticity is complicated because the cloud clones instances, and there is little or no customization (e.g., assign IP) that happens when a host is cloned.

Before moving an application in a public cloud, it should be customized for the cloud. There are many things that need to be adjusted; the following are just some recommendations to address security and privacy-related concerns:

- Encryption keys should be stored outside the cloud environment (HMS/VPC clouds allow for the storage in either a hardware crypto module provided by the CMS or in your own IT environment).

- Memory routines should ensure that memory that is being used for sensitive information (e.g., passwords) is wiped by the application, and it is not relying on the OS to wipe the memory.
- Logging needs to be done to a centralized server, not local, to ensure that logging information stays available once an instance of the VM is decommissioned.
- Any logging that uses IP addresses for identification of the host must be adjusted to use the host name. IP addresses do not mean much in the public cloud.
- The application should support the metering that the cloud offers to ensure that the CSP properly bills you for the cloud resources being used.
- Applications must be adjusted to allow for "many-to-many" communication. In most cases the cloud handles this with load balancers. However, the servers and applications sitting behind those load balancers need to be aware of these many-to-many relationships to properly function in the cloud.
- Applications using fancy ways to facilitate network communication will be difficult to adapt to a cloud environment. When I say fancy, I am referring to some homegrown load balancing or the spoofing of IPs or anything else that goes beyond normal transmission control protocol (TCP) or user datagram protocol (UDP) communication with the host IP. The CSP will not very likely allow you to use this fancy communication since part of their security controls is to tightly control the IP allocation. Otherwise, it would be impossible to shape and control the flow of network traffic in a public cloud.

3

BEFORE YOU DECIDE
TO OUTSOURCE

The question "What are the risks?" is not easily answered and has more aspects to it than just from a security perspective: for example, how agile does my IT need to be to support our business? Companies that need flexibility in how IT supports their business will have a hard time finding an outsourcing company that actually can (and I mean not one that only commits to it in their Statement of Work) keep up with their demand for the ever-changing IT infrastructure. Reality is that changes to the IT infrastructure have now another bureaucratic layer, when outsourced, in the form of Service Level Agreements (SLAs), contract terms, change orders, and so forth. This is widely underestimated and maybe even ignored by managers that make the final decision to outsource or not.

Outsourcing is like giving up a hand-tailored suit that fits like nothing else. Most companies will not achieve this "right fit" by outsourcing parts or all of IT. It might result in a more mature IT environment with less cost, but it needs to be understood that this will be more akin to the suit off the rack with some slight modifications than the handmade IT-Armani suit that every chief information officer dreams of.

Security and Privacy Impacts

When outsourcing business processes or IT, security is impacted at various levels. Information that used to reside in a controlled environment, physically as well as logically, is passed on to a third party that is now entrusted with protecting the information against unauthorized access and corruption (intentionally or unintentionally) and with making it available to the business whenever it is needed. To add to these requirements, now your organization needs to make sure that the outsourcing company is trustworthy and executes as agreed on in the contract both parties signed. Critical pieces of information that ensure that your organization is competitive (e.g., the Coca-Cola recipe) or your personnel files with Personal Protected Information (PPI) are now accessible by the outsourcing company's personnel. Information that is protected by laws and regulations in various states and countries around the globe becomes an SLA with the outsourcing company. The level of criticality of particular information is maybe passed on to the outsourcing company in a signed contract, but down the road the information is just one piece among many. Furthermore, the outsourcing industry has adopted a model of cascading outsourcing that has resulted in some of the services not being provided by the original outsourcing company but by a third party that the outsourcing company has contracted to provide certain services to the outsourcing company. This third party might have another fourth party that provides services to them involving your data. It is very unlikely that those additional service providers understand your requirements for security and privacy of the information that you entrusted to the original outsourcing company. This results in a situation where nobody can understand the complete picture anymore. Information that should have been hosted only in the United States suddenly winds up in India or other countries. With the introduction of cloud-based outsourcing offerings, this situation has now become even more complex since many cloud service providers (CSPs) use technologies that allow for cloud bursting, which can mean that additional cloud resources are added from other geographical regions. Cloud bursting can also mean that your private cloud suddenly has resources added from a public cloud. The visibility to the information owner is taken away more and more.

Secure Communication

The sooner you think about secure communication in the outsourcing deal, the faster you get one of the biggest information leakage areas under control. Communication is going to take place at various levels of the organizations and in various formats. Phone, e-mail, instant messaging, paper, and videoconferencing are just some of the modern ways that we use to communicate with each other. The problem is that those ways of communicating are not always secure. Particularly after the revelations of Edward Snowden, who was not the first, pointing out that globally there are governments eavesdropping on all forms of communication. The PRISM program is probably the most famous, controlled by the National Security Agency (NSA) however, it is not the only program in place. I say this because with outsourcing deals the communication takes place at a global level. Only if both endpoints and the communication channel are secure can the information that is communicated stay secure. Secure can mean it stays confidential, or the integrity of the information stays intact, or the communication can take place and is available to you.

Telephones

The telephone is one of the oldest forms of communication. In the early days of telephone service, so-called party lines were in place. A couple of neighbors shared one phone line. It was expected that when a party realized that the call was not for them, they would hang up. So much for that theory. In reality human curiosity resulted in neighbors sometimes listening to each other's conversations. Not to mention that the operator who had to manually patch calls through could easily listen in to calls. Nowadays we have telephone service nearly everywhere. Landlines are dying a slow death with a generation of college graduates simply relying on their mobile phones and having no need for a landline anymore. Times have changed, but not human curiosity or the fear of missing out on a detail that could be terrorism related or in some cases be used for corporate espionage. So-called signals intelligence (SIGINT)-gathering systems are capable of gathering information from satellite communication, microwave links (as used by telephone companies to bridge long distances), wireless services (cell phone service) and cordless phones. ECHELON is one system that performs SIGINT by collecting and analyzing worldwide communication. The ECHELON network is operated on behalf of five countries (Australia, Canada, New Zealand, the United Kingdom, and the United States) according to the UKUSA Security Agreement.[*] ECHELON was originally created to monitor

---

[*] http://www.nsa.gov/public_info/press_room/2010/ukusa.shtml.

the military and diplomatic communications of the Soviet Union and its Eastern Bloc allies during the Cold War in the early 1960s. The European Parliament formed a committee during 2000 and 2001 to investigate ECHELON and issued a report in 2001. The report stated that the ECHELON is used in a number of contexts but that evidence indicates that ECHELON stands for a signals intelligence collection system. This investigation uncovers an interesting situation with the UK, which is part of the European Union (EU) and is also actively involved with ECHELON. It is suspected that the five member countries have divided up the monitoring responsibilities.

- **Australia** eavesdrops for communication that originates in Indochina, Indonesia, and southern China.
- **Canada** used to monitor the northern portions of the former Soviet Union and conducted sweeps of all forms of communication that could be picked up from embassies around the world. After the Cold War era ended, the focus shifted to monitoring satellite, radio, and cell phone traffic originating from Central and South America to track drugs and non-aligned paramilitary groups in that region.
- **New Zealand** is targeting the western Pacific with listening stations in the South Island at Waihopai Valley and on the North Island at Tangimoana. Locals hold regular protests against the listening posts, demanding that they be closed down.
- **United Kingdom** is responsible for monitoring communication in Europe, Africa, and the European part of Russia. There have been cases in which companies located in non-ECHELON participating countries suspected that the ECHELON system was used to provide UK- or US-based companies a competitive advantage by passing recorded information to companies in their countries.
- **United States** monitors most of Latin America, Asia, Asiatic Russia, and northern China.

The report issued by the EU also concludes that ECHELON was capable of eavesdropping on and analyzing telephone calls, faxes, e-mail, and other data traffic that traverse via satellite transmission, microwave links, and public-switched telephone networks (carrying Internet traffic during the early stages of the Internet revolution). It has been suspected for quite some time that ECHELON is used not only to protect the national security of the five member states but also for industrial espionage. Germany's national intelligence agency, Verfassungsschutz, has warned German businesses and the German industry community against ECHELON since June 1999, when it recommended that German companies encrypt all important information—encode it to prevent ECHELON stations from picking up the communication and using it to their advantage. The Verfassungsschutz even issued in 2008 a brochure* to German companies providing guidance on how to protect sensitive information, not mentioning ECHELON but clearly stating that communication can be eavesdropped on.

e-Mail

In the early days of e-mail communication, the e-mail servers exchanged the content of e-mails in clear text across the Internet. Since these early days, this has changed, and many e-mail servers now offer secure transmission of e-mails via the Transport Layer Security (TLS), the successor of the Secure Sockets Layer (SSL) protocol. This allows for secure communication between e-mail servers. To check if TLS is in place, you can inspect the full-header of an e-mail that contains the server handshake part. If the header contains a line like this (or similar—the keyword is TLS), "(version = TLSv1 cipher = RC4-SHA bits = 128/128)," then TLS version 1 was used to secure the communication from one e-mail server to another. One caveat to the above line, the RC4 cipher† is no longer considered secure, and an e-mail server should not use the RC4 stream cipher algorithm anymore. A prominent victim of the weakness of RC4 was the Wired Equivalent Privacy (WEP) protocol that is nowadays considered highly insecure. Too often individuals (particular auditors) seem to check only for the word TLS in the header of an e-mail and do not actually pay attention to the actual cipher that is being used. With computing power doubling every two to three years (see Moore's

---

* http://www.verfassungsschutz.de/de/oeffentlichkeitsarbeit/publikationen/ pb-spionage-und-proliferationsabwehr/broschuere-4-0806-wirtschaftsspionage (in German).

† http://www.schneier.com/blog/archives/2013/03/new_rc4_attack.html

law*), a weak crypto algorithm can easily result in no obstacle at all after just a couple of months or years.

In the United States and in Europe, the governments are actively discussing the storage of information about communication that takes place using e-mail, social media, or telephone. The approaches that the EU and the United States are pursuing vary. The EU approach in general only requires the storage of envelope information of an e-mail but not the actual content of the e-mail. The actual interpretation and implementation of the EU directive have varied by country. The United States, on the other hand, has implemented measures that go beyond what the EU has defined. After the 9/11 attacks, a shift took place in how anonymity and privacy of e-mails are handled in the United States. Intelligence agencies have been using intelligent software that can screen the content of millions of e-mails with relative ease (e.g., NSA's XKeyscore[†] goes even beyond e-mails). Civil rights activists heavily criticize the practice of screening e-mails. Agencies such as the US Federal Bureau of Investigation conduct screening operations regularly. The American Civil Liberties Union and other organizations alleged that Verizon illegally gave the US government unrestricted access to its entire Internet traffic without a warrant and that AT&T had a similar arrangement with the NSA. In 2008, Congress passed the FISA Amendments Act of 2008 (FAA) granting AT&T and Verizon immunity from any prosecution. According to a whistleblower (William Binney, a former NSA employee), the NSA has collected over 20 trillion communications, including many e-mail communications.

Mobile/Cell Phones

As already mentioned in the telephone section, governments around the world are spying on wireless and wired communication, no matter where you are. Since the new millennium (potentially earlier), companies like ThorpeGlen, VASTech, Kommlabs, and Aqsacom sell so-called passive probing data-mining services to governments around

---

[*] http://www.merriam-webster.com/dictionary/moore's%20law
[†] http://www.theguardian.com/world/2013/jul/31/nsa-top-secret-program-online-data

the world, according to a *London Review of Books* article.[*] For example, ThorpeGlen, a UK-based vendor, provides mobile phone location and call records via its data-mining software. The sky seems to be the limit when it comes to analysis of data gathered: a target's community of interest, a single person swapping SIM cards, or even throwing away phones—no problem.

Smartphones

The success of smartphones around the globe is unprecedented. Particularly the younger generation has adopted this new technology, using it wherever they can: e-mail, text (SMS), one-time access code applications, and so forth. Unfortunately, smartphones have become the target not only of criminals but also governments, which want to control any information that might go against the regime in that country. Western countries use "government spyware" on smartphones, too. One company that has tapped into this market is Gamma International, a UK-based company marketing a spyware called FinFisher, under the description "IT intrusion and remote monitoring solution." FinFisher is supposedly only offered to law enforcement and intelligence agencies to covertly monitor criminals. However, according to researchers, it has been used by repressive regimes, for example, by the Bahraini government to spy on dissidents. According to some analysis, a demo version of the FinFisher software was in some cases reverse-engineered to a certain degree removing the demo mode limitations. FinFisher is available in versions that work on mobile phones of all major brands. FinFisher has the ability to take control of target smartphones and capture even encrypted data and communications. Using "enhanced remote deployment methods" it can install software on target smartphones.

FinFisher is, at the current time, the crème de la crème of spyware for smartphones (and computers). However, many other security issues might put your sensitive information at risk. For example, in late 2012 a research team at the University of Leipzig, Germany, discovered that the SSL implementation,[†] used by many applications on the popular Android platform, is insecure.

---

[*] http://www.lrb.co.uk/v30/n16/daniel-soar/short-cuts.
[†] http://www2.dcsec.uni-hannover.de/files/android/p50-fahl.pdf.

In another case, free smartphone applications that were using an advertisement framework to generate revenue for the usage of the application were introducing malware through the advertisement framework.*

Many other threats make smartphone platforms potentially unsuitable for highly sensitive data.

BlackBerrys

Probably still the most secure smartphone platform available is the BlackBerry. Even Research in Motion (RIM), the manufacturer of BlackBerrys, had to give in to demands from the Indian government (and others) to allow it to eavesdrop on communication taking place using the BlackBerry encryption. RIM demonstrated in August 2012 a solution developed by a firm called Verint that can intercept messages and e-mails exchanged between BlackBerry handsets. This solution makes encrypted communications available in a readable format to Indian security agencies. Many experts doubt the validity of the claim of the Indian government that it uses the eavesdropping to identify terrorism. It is suspected that the Indian government uses the intelligence gathered from the business-to-business communication (this is the only communication that RIM had encrypted) for other purposes.

Instant Messenger

It is not a well-known fact that instant messaging (IM) predates the Internet. Early versions of instant messaging appeared already in multiuser operating systems like Compatible Time-Sharing System (CTSS) and Multiplexed Information and Computing Service (Multics) in the mid-1960s. Later when network connectivity became more widely available, some new protocols came up, some of them using peer-to-peer protocols (e.g., talk, ntalk and ytalk) and others having a client-server architecture (e.g., Internet Relay Chat [IRC]). Many IM solutions followed. However, America Online (AOL)

---

* http://www.csoonline.com/article/732204/bogus-ad-network-marks-new-twist-
on-android-malware.

offered the first IM that had huge success, with millions of users still using it today. The AOL Instant Messenger (AIM) has been leading the way for modern IM solutions (Google Talk, Yahoo IM, Microsoft Messenger, etc.) offering not only a text chat function but nowadays also voice chat, video chat, and file transfer function. As useful as IM solutions are—boosting productivity, particularly for teams that are geographically dispersed—they also carry a high risk if they are implemented by using one of the public IM offerings (Yahoo, AOL, Microsoft, Google, etc.). The following could be considered the top five risks and liabilities:

- **Malware infections through IM**—IM networks have been used to deliver large numbers of phishing links (i.e., URLs) and file attachments containing malware. Even if your computer is not the direct target of an attack, the user around the globe could not run antivirus software on their computer and would get infected with malware.
- **Compliance issues**—In the United States alone there are more than 10,000 laws and regulations related to electronic communication and records retention. Some of the well-known ones include the Sarbanes–Oxley Act (SOX), the Health Insurance Portability and Accountability Act (HIPAA), and SEC 17a-3 requiring that certain exchange members are required to create records in a certain way. For example, in December 2007 the Financial Industry Regulatory Authority (FINRA) issued to member firms in the financial services industry a clarification stating that the terms *electronic communications*, *e-mail*, and *electronic correspondence* may be used interchangeably and do include electronic messaging as instant messaging and text messaging. This ruling states that companies that are required to be in compliance with it record IM and text messages since many IM communications fall into the category of business communications, which must be archived and retrievable according to SEC 17a-3.
- **Requiring additional ports**—Unfortunately, due to the nature of IM, running behind firewalls, or on networks using network address translation (NAT), the programmers of some

IM applications have been creative in keeping a communication channel open to the IM server. This sometimes involves the User Datagram Protocol (UDP) network protocol. UDP is not known for its security and allows for spoofing of communication sources.

- **Social engineering**—Just like the traditional form of social engineering, IM has been used to claim the identity of someone to gather information. Sometimes the IM name varies by only one character, using the limitations of character sets. For example, I and 1 or O and 0 are often swapped for each other to create an IM name that on the first glance looks like the name of a trusted person.

- **Leakage of confidential information**—IM applications usually use communication protocols that are in plain text, making them vulnerable to eavesdropping attacks. Another area of concern is that many IM protocols are not peer-to-peer protocols but traverse through servers of the company offering the free IM solutions. There have been many speculations why this is being done since it creates a cost overhead for the company offering the free service to the public.

IM has been widely used by outsourcing companies; however, the risks that the usage of IM introduces must meet up with your risk appetite and compliance requirements.

Letters and Parcels

The old-fashioned way to transport information from point A to point B, using a carrier that provides tracking of your shipment, can give you a false sense of security. Yes, you know where your letter or parcel is; however, tracking does not help much when the letter or parcel has been delivered to the wrong address and the signature is completely unreadable or no signature has been recorded. In most cases international shipments require additional paperwork, such as customs forms that need to be filled out. In some countries, parcels or larger envelopes are routinely opened and inspected. Those inspections serve different purposes, depending on how stable the regime is in a certain country.

Organizational Impacts

Outsourcing companies offer solutions that would allow a chief executive officer to have a whole company operate by buying only outsourcing services. Ranging from the technical staff up to the management team, everything and everyone can be outsourced nowadays. Outsourcing companies have become quite sophisticated in their offerings, building a pool of staff that can provide nearly any service your company might need. But what does that really mean? It means that your company has to put additional measures in place to address individuals employed by a third party having access to buildings, servers, files, information, and more.

Legal Aspects

The local law is what is applicable to the operation of a corporation. Large multinational organizations know this. However, if you are a national corporation that maybe operates in only a handful of states in the United States, you might not be familiar with how local law can vary from country to country. For example, outsourcing to India will allow the Indian government to gain access to the systems that your organization uses in India and might contain confidential information. It is critical that before any contract is put in place, a lawyer with expertise in international law and outsourcing initiatives provides you with guidance and does a final review of a complex outsourcing contract. The protection of intellectual property (IP) is not unified across the globe, and it would not be the first time that a local company in the country where you have your outsourced operation suddenly has inside knowledge of what your organization has kept as a well-protected secret for years. Particularly countries like China are known for problems with the protection of IP owned by foreign corporations.

Personnel Issues

Not everyone who is working for an outsourcing company cheats and steals. Just to clarify a rumor that has been going around: Large outsourcing companies have a stringent background investigation process, which is not perfect, but most of the time ensures that the companies hire only law-abiding and upright people. However, a salary at the lower end of the scale and some temptations can result in a situation that you might have never experienced before, such as theft of computer equipment or information. Taking additional measures like requesting additional background checks or drug screening is advisable when sensitive information or critical systems are involved. At the same time disgruntled employees of your own organization can pose a threat to your organization. For years those employees had worked for your organization, passed the background check before being hired, and are now out to hurt the organization one way or another.

Technical Challenges

This section is a little technology heavy, diving into some of the quickly overlooked foot traps that outsourcing can bring with it. For the purpose of this section, a Technology Outsourcing (TO) engagement is assumed with a client that is going to outsource its IT infrastructure.

Network Address Translation (NAT) Issues

In some cases you will have your existing network tied into the network of the outsourcing provider. This setup usually brings challenges with it since in some cases address collisions can happen. For example, if your organization uses a 192.168.2.0/24 network and the outsourcing company uses the same address range, you will need to implement NAT. This usually creates a very messy network setup that is not easily understood or troubleshot anymore—not to mention network security such as network intrusion detection systems, which will need to be retrained or reconfigured to reflect the new network setup and traffic on the network.

Single Sign-On and Federation (SAML/XACML)

The problem of allowing a user to use one login for all the IT systems they need to fulfill their job function is not new. It gets even more complex when two organizations have a mixed workforce that needs to access systems in both organizations. Not only login credentials but also the access rights that each user requires need to be shared across organizational borders. SAML and XACML have been presented as the silver bullets to address those issues. This sounds simple; however, the problem is more complex, since access can be given based on various methodologies: role based, group based, entitlement based, etc. If each organization has a different approach to how access is given, you will very likely have a huge challenge at hand in providing the right access to the right people. To solve this problem can easily fill a book by itself.

Backup Technologies

There have been many backup technologies and standards over the years. Organizations bought into a vendor or standard at one point in time. Now that this task gets transitioned to an outsourcing company, this could mean that the company has its own standard that it uses for all of its clients. Once it transitions and the old backup solution is decommissioned, your organization might be at risk of falling out of compliance if you are required to have a certain number of years of data available. When the outsourcing company has provided the service for a number of years, you are back in compliance, but between decommissioning your old backup solution, which might no longer be available on the market, and the new backups having caught up to the number of years or months that are required by a regulation, you are at risk.

Remote Desktop Support

With having support teams in sometimes faraway countries, the remote desktop support solution that used to work is now not working anymore. Network latency prevents any meaningful network communication between the computer of the support personnel and the user that has a problem with their computer.

Trouble Ticket Systems

Larger or even midsize outsourcing companies will have their own trouble ticket system (e.g., Remedy, osTicket, to name just two), often referred to as a *ticketing system*. Usually those trouble ticket systems do not talk to each other. Some might offer interfaces to import or export certain message formats, but even with that it can be tricky to have two systems talk to each other. So when keeping your own ticketing system, it might be challenging to have tickets cross over to the out-sourcing company's trouble ticketing system. Problems that can occur are date and time differences when importing (import might happen in a foreign destination, or simply the import corrupts the ticket), which can result in a problem in determining if a specific SLA was met or not. In other cases some proprietary fields of a ticket do not map to the other system's fields. There can be a large number of sources for errors, depending on which systems are talking to each other. The effort to fix those issues can be so high that it takes months before it is working reliably. In the meantime the outsourcing company will have someone take tickets out of your trouble ticket system and retype them into the outsourcing company's trouble ticket system. This can easily introduce human error or mess up the SLA calculation completely.

Business Continuity

How does this new relationship survive a natural disaster like a hur-ricane? The overall picture of business continuity and its dependencies suddenly have become quite complex. There is probably not one com-pany that I can think of that does not have a dependency on another company so it is able to conduct its business. However, most of them have some level of flexibility built into that dependency, such as diesel generators that are available when the power to the data center fails. The diesel tanks are usually full and allow operating for several hours or sometimes days, even with diesel fuel not being available. Those are relatively straightforward relationships that can be addressed. With the level of outsourcing nowadays, even mission-critical pro-cesses and functions are outsourced. Sometimes the outsourcing com-pany further outsources certain elements of its operation; e.g., many Indian outsourcing companies were using workers in Egypt for their internal support functions, as they were cheaper than the local Indian workforce. When the Arab spring started, the Egyptian govern-ment blocked all Internet access to outside of the country, impacting the operation of Indian outsourcing companies delivering service in North America. I think this example illustrates how complex these dependencies have become in a global economy. To understand this, someone would need to understand the whole picture. Unfortunately, this is nearly impossible with the complexity in place, and it is rather a common practice to have the outsourcing company prove that it has conducted its business continuity exercise. On the other hand, the business continuity exercises that most outsourcing companies conduct have only limited input from the clients they serve.

4
READY TO OUTSOURCE

Most organizations have established a well-defined appetite for risk when doing business. Outsourcing parts or the majority of the business functions holds significant risk since it is a game changer for some traditional security and privacy controls, requiring a new approach in how to achieve an acceptable risk level.

Perfect Outsourcing Company

So what would be the perfect outsourcing company? What would it have to offer, and who would be the people behind it? To be clear, there is no perfect outsourcing company out there. There might be an outsourcing company that is a better match for your organization and others that are less of a match. For sure you will need to compromise. A perfect outsourcing company would significantly cut your operational costs, bring your capital expenditures to zero, and have the smartest people you have ever seen working for it. Outsourcing companies might use a similar pitch. However, those companies using that pitch should be more a warning to you than anything else.

Doing Your Homework

So now that we know the perfect outsourcing company does not exist, what do we need to do to find the best match for the needs of your organization? To be able to make the right decision on whether to outsource and to determine what to outsource and what to keep in house, we need to be able to ask the right questions and gather the necessary information. A company requiring agility with its IT services might not be able to go with a standard outsourcing offering and might need some time to find the right partner. Nowadays partnerships in the sense of corporations taking ownership stakes in outsourcing companies are not unusual anymore; still it is no guarantee for success either. To really understand a particular outsourcing company's capabilities, organizations need to do quite a lot of homework. Too many companies jumped on the bandwagon called outsourcing. And someone might be surprised in what the organization bought into once they have had their first visit to the offshore facility of the outsourcing company. There are several aspects that can be used as indicators for the security capabilities of an outsourcing company:

1. *Corporate culture* (not maturity level as the Capability Maturity Model Integration [CMMI] program understands it)—What is the average turnover rate within the organization? With most organizations that have a high turnover rate, there is usually an underlying problem, a problem that you might inherit when hiring the company. A human resources department that is overworked with on- and off-boarding of resources, or a workforce that is inexperienced in executing mature processes and unknown to the "new guy/gal" hired three weeks ago. A high turnover rate also results in people bringing their own ways and opinion of doing things. This is OK when you are looking for innovation; however, if the organization just consists of new hires with few "old-timers" around, it will have issues in functioning well. The same goes for companies that grew mainly by merger and acquisitions. They usually have a hard time building a corporate culture.

2. *Subcontractor ratio*—Another aspect to look at with an outsourcing company. If an outsourcing company on average has a two-to-one subcontractor ratio, then the contractual overhead is a major challenge, not to mention the work culture aspect (see point above). If those subcontractors are even different across the various outsourcing engagements, it is questionable if issues can be resolved in a reasonable time and with reasonable involvement of resources (e.g., contract personnel researching, lawyers being the next level if no resolution can be found). Each outsourcing company will have a number of subcontractors supporting the effort, particularly if there are some "hand-tailored" items that are unique to your orga-

nization; still it creates a level of complexity that is usually underestimated.

3. *Ability to implement/enforce security processes and standards*—This has always been a challenge across organizational boundaries. With an outsourcing organization it becomes even more critical. What does the outsourcing organization offer for training, enforcement, documentation, and evidence collection? Is the organization well familiar with security controls, or is this done as a "must do"? An outsourcing organization might need to have audits conducted to be in compliance. This does not mean that those controls are the same as those you require; sometimes those controls are at a different level than yours. So your controls would need to be added or supersede the outsourcing company's controls. In any case, controls are only as good as the people who are responsible for them.

4. *Level of standardization of IT*—What does the outsourcing organization have in place? Many outsourcing organizations have the tendency to "grab" whatever deal they can get, claiming the ability to support any technology. Yes, you could go the route of transformation with your environment, but that could easily cost you more than running it on your own. So most of the time the outsourcing company takes your technology and incorporates it into their environment. If you use technology that is not standardized, you will easily fall into the trap of losing experienced staff, and you suddenly have a quite inexperienced outsourcing staff trying to maintain this specialized piece of technology. The outsourcing companies usually have IT staff cross-trained in various technologies; still you will hardly find a Windows administrator that is also a full-fledged UNIX administrator. Another aspect is cost; UNIX administrators are usually paid higher than Windows administrators. To keep costs low, the outsourcing company is constantly trying to minimize the need for more human resources and maximize the utilization of the existing staff. There is not much room for resources with specialized skills.

5. *Process maturity (e.g., CMMI)*—Usually used by outsourcing organizations for advertisement. In reality those organizations might have achieved a certain CMMI level within a

certain part of the organization. This does not mean that suddenly your organization, that has struggled to even achieve CMMI level 2, will see a boost in process maturity. Also the opposite holds true—an outsourcing company that has a lower level of process maturity than yours will very likely struggle to execute at a higher maturity level that your organization might have achieved.

6. *Average time of background investigations*—This can vary quite a bit across countries. A background investigation taking three months or longer is not unusual in certain countries. Outsourcing companies are looking for cheap labor, and most of the countries that are used to find resources to staff the next engagement have problematic background investigations. Another factor is the rate of background investigations that result in firing someone who has already been hired (i.e., the resume was fake) or in a delay in onboarding the individuals. All those are metrics that go to the core of human resources, and most outsourcing companies will not openly share those with you. If this is the case, job boards (e.g., Glassdoor) sometimes can paint a picture of what is going on with a particular outsourcing company. Another approach is to get some larger and smaller customers of the outsourcing organization (all with the permission of the outsourcing organization) to talk with you.

7. *Ability to map your security architecture to the new outsourced company environment*—Building a security architecture that works from soup to nuts can take years. To push this into a virtualized environment or even further into a cloud environment can result in a serious setback. Metrics that are not available anymore, and security controls and processes that need to be adjusted to a potential new environment resulting in gaps. There was a reason why your organization did not go with vendor B when it came to network intrusion prevention/detection system (IPS/IDS). The outsourcing company might have chosen vendor B for their data center network intrusion detection needs. It is unrealistic to believe that an outsourcing company will install your vendor A product in a shared data center at choke points where IDS/IPS usually are located.

This is particularly true for IPS since those actively try to prevent a network intrusion. The money and time that your organization invested in researching, evaluating, and eventually implementing and tweaking such an IPS might be lost.

8. *Vendor relationships*—Another critical aspect of how good outsourcing companies can address your needs. Most of the larger outsourcing companies have close ties to vendors that provide solutions to them (this sometimes goes hand in hand with the subcontractor situation and the level of standardization of IT). Outsourcing organizations have created those close ties to gain discounts with certain vendors. The worst question you can pose to an outsourcing company is their recommendation for a replacement of a particular piece of software that is not directly supported by them. The answer will very likely be Vendor ABC, one of the vendors that they have a strategic relationship with. This can also be a benefit, if you already are using that particular piece of software; however, most of the time you will find yourself with a recommendation that is driven by the overall direction to just recommend the vendors that are preferred or even part of an alliance with the outsourcing company.

9. *Ability to understand your business*—This is critical for the success of outsourcing engagements that go beyond IT (i.e., server gets moved to an outsourcing data center). It starts with the help desk, which usually is part of IT outsourcing engagements, and can be as simple as cultural issues. For example, Joe working in the trenches, laying pipes in the ground, and having to use a laptop to provide update reports to his boss, back in the office. This guy is very likely not pleased with having to deal with someone over the phone, who potentially has an accent and is not accustomed to American slang. Another level is business processes that might be critical to your business. If the outsourcing company has a good understanding of your business, potentially also works with one of your competitors, then they will ensure that those processes get the appropriate attention and urgency. Most of the time the outsourcing company has some personnel allocated across various outsourcing engagements. Those individuals will have a

hard time adjusting to the nuances of your processes, working sometimes 2–3 different client engagements.

10. *Ability to separate your environment from a competitor*—Another critical factor. There have been cases where information was available to a competitor who was also using the same outsourcing company. Whether those two companies were always aware of the situation is another question. However, it can be critical to your company to have intellectual property protected against unauthorized access.

Those are just some of the more important factors that should be considered when picking an outsourcing company. In the end, your organization will need to come up with your own evaluation criteria that align with your business, your systems, process, and more importantly, your risk tolerance.

Understand What Is Offered

It is one thing to understand what is needed; it is another thing to understand what is offered. Nowadays outsourcing companies offer a wide variety of services. Believing the marketing and sales departments of the outsourcing companies makes you think that the sky is the limit. Unfortunately this does not necessarily align with the delivery capabilities that those companies really have. Some of them might try to use you as the guinea pig for the latest (sometimes not even production-ready) offering. Margins are small in the outsourcing industry, and a solution that might slice off another dollar or two is interesting for anyone in the outsourcing industry. Do not use outsourcing to finally try the quantum jump that senior management has been dreaming of for quite some time. There is no issue with transforming sections of IT or the business that work with rather antiquated methods or equipment to a robust state-of-the-art solution. You will be busy enough with just moving your existing environment into the outsourcing environment.

Audit Reports

It is a good idea to ask for an audit report from an outsourcing company to get a better understanding of the security controls they have implemented to protect their customers' information. However, there are many auditing standards out there, with at least three current report types and one retired one (SAS-70, retired in June 2011), so it is important to understand which one to ask for. No matter what type of report you are going to look at, it is important to understand that the reports (SOC 1 or SOC 2) represent only the opinion of an auditor and are not a certification of any kind. The only certification currently is SOC 3.

Trust Services—SysTrust and WebTrust The need for Trust Services, such as SysTrust and WebTrust, has grown exponentially in recent years, due to the growth of e-commerce and the overall e-business environment, resulting in large amounts of sensitive and confidential data that is processed and stored by service organizations like outsourcing companies. SysTrust/WebTrust audit and assurance services are a set of principles and criteria defined by the American Institute of Certified Public Accountants and the Canadian Institute of Chartered Accountants.

Qualified or Unqualified Auditors like to use a certain lingo in their reports, which sometimes can be confusing to nonauditors. Sometimes the verbiage used comes from the early days of financial auditing and sometimes does not "stretch" to IT audits. For example the use of *unqualified opinion*, *qualified opinion*, *adverse opinion*, and *disclaimer of opinion* in a report can easily be mistaken for the opposite of what they really stand for. Let's take a look at what they really mean:

- *Unqualified opinion*—An unqualified opinion states that the auditor concludes that, for example, the financial statements are accurate according to the financial reporting framework used for their preparation and presentation. To clarify, an unqualified opinion is what you want to see when looking at an audit report provided by an outsourcing company.
- *Qualified opinion*—On the other hand an auditor qualifying their opinion can mean that the auditor encountered one of two types of situations that deviate from generally accepted accounting principles; however, the rest of the financial statements are stated according to the financial reporting frame-

work. A limited scope or a single deviation in a particular area of financial reporting can result in a qualified opinion.

- *Adverse opinion*—This opinion is issued when the auditor determines that the financial statements of an organization are materially misstated and, when considered as a whole, do not conform to the financial reporting framework. An adverse opinion is considered the opposite of an unqualified or clean opinion, stating that the information gathered or provided is materially incorrect, unreliable, and inaccurate, making it impossible to assess the financial position and results of the organization.
- *Disclaimer of opinion*—Commonly referred to simply as a disclaimer, this is issued when the auditor could not form and consequently refuses to provide an opinion on the financial statements. This opinion is issued when the auditor tried to audit an organization but could not complete the work and does not want to issue an opinion due to lack of information.

Type 1 and Type 2 Reports   A Type 1 report represents the auditor's opinion regarding the accuracy and completeness of management's description of the system or service as well as the suitability of the design of controls as on a specific date (point-of-time audit). On the other hand, a Type 2 report includes not only the point-of-time view but also the operating effectiveness of the controls throughout a declared time period. The time period can vary between 6 and 12 months. So a Type 2 report usually provides a more complete picture; not only does it comment on if and how an outsourcing company has security controls implemented but also how they are operated over a specific time.

SSAE 16 (SOC 1)/SOC 2/SOC 3   So what audit standards are commonly available and which one do I need to ask for when evaluating an outsourcing company? Below is an overview of the three main audit standards that are used with service organizations in the United States. There are corresponding international standards (Figure 4.1).

SSAE 16 (SOC 1)   SSAE 16 stands for Statement on Standards for Attestation Engagements (SSAE) No. 16. SSAE 16 was issued by the Auditing Standards Board of the American Institute of Certified Public Accountants in April 2010 and allows for reporting on controls

Overview of Service Organization Audit Types			
Type of Audit:	Service Org Control 1 (SOC 1)	Service Org Control 2 (SOC 2)	Service Org Control 3 (SOC 3)
Based on:	SSAE16	AT 101	AT 101
Restrictions:	Restricted Use Report (Type 1 or 2)	Generally a Restricted Use Report (Type 1 or 2)	General Use Report (contains public seal)
Scope:	Reports on controls with financial statement audits	Reports on controls related to compliance or operations	Reports on controls related to compliance or operations

Figure 4.1 Overview of service organization audits.

that are part of financial reporting of a service organization. SSAE 16 can be considered the direct successor of SAS-70 audit standard, which provided a means of reporting on internal controls over financial reporting. An SSAE 16 is also sometimes referred to as an SOC 1 audit. Compared with the old SAS-70 standard, the SSAE 16 standard has an increased scope, including a baseline of controls that a service provider is required to implement. The old SAS-70 standard looked only at the controls that the service provider had implemented. This limitation resulted in reports that could not be compared between service providers since the number of implemented controls could vary quite a bit. SOC 1 audits can be of a Type 1 or a Type 2.

SOC 2 An SOC 2 audit provides much more stringent audit requirements than an SOC 1. SOC 2 reports are conducted in accordance with the American Institute of Certified Public Accountants' standard for attestation (AT) Standard Section 101, using a predefined set of controls and requirements specifically designed around data center service organizations. An SOC 2 allows for the comparison of two data center audits using the same set of criteria and a standard benchmark. This is in contrast to an SSAE 16 engagement, where the data center operator defines the criteria for an audit. The SOC 2 audit standard uses a predefined Trust Services Principles and Criteria model built around security, availability, process integrity, privacy, and confidentiality. This allows for an assessment of the safeguards that the service provider has in place to safeguard data and information of their clients. SOC 2 audits, like the SOC 1 audits, can be either of a Type 1 or a Type 2.

SOC 3   SOC 3 reports state if a service organization's systems meet the SOC 2 criteria but do not describe the actual tests or results achieved. It is the only audit that results in a certification (with a public seal). Like SOC 2 the focus with SOC 3 audits is to ensure that security, availability, processing integrity, confidentiality, or privacy risks are properly addressed according to AT Section 101. SOC 3 meets the demand that has been requested, for quite some time, a certification. When an auditor is assured that the service organization has achieved the trust services criteria, the organization can then display the SOC 3 SysTrust for service organizations seal. The SysTrust seal can be displayed on the organization's website for one full calendar year from the date of issue. After that the SOC 3 audit needs to be renewed. Only certified public accountant (CPA) firms can issue the certification.

Is Business Transformation Outsourcing the Right Choice?

If your organization has realized that your business has fallen behind with key technologies, outsourcing companies might offer a Business Transformation Outsourcing (BTO) deal. Part of such a deal could be, for example, to move the majority of your IT operation into the cloud. In that case you might have to develop a new set of security controls that addresses the new threats and vulnerabilities of a cloud operation. Going through that exercise, you can put controls in three categories: ones that can be moved from a traditional IT environment into the cloud (e.g., host-level IDS with an Internet as a Service Cloud); others that cannot be put into the cloud and would need to be replaced or are no longer applicable (e.g., network segmentation, network firewalls); and finally, new controls that address cloud-specific threats and vulnerabilities (e.g., host-level encryption). No matter what the BTO solution looks like, it will very likely require a reevaluation of the existing control framework and security architecture. So what can BTO do for an organization? The answer is, it depends. It can mean that consultants will come in and analyze what you do and propose a new implementation, way of doing things, with the outsourcing company implementing and running it. Or it can result in your solutions being replaced by whatever solution is favored by the outsourcing company. In many cases it means that the outsourcing company has a strategic relationship with a vendor, promising the vendor that each transformation deal that the outsourcing company wins has a piece for the vendor in it. What is in it for the outsourcing company? The outsourcing company gets significant discounts that are partially passed on to the client. So this could be seen as a win-win for all parties involved. However, the potential for cost savings can have an outsourcing company trying to force a solution, which is not always in your best interest.

Ask the Right Questions

Even with transforming an antiquated solution, some confirmation from the outsourcing company should be gained that they have the necessary experience and are able to maintain the new solution. The following are questions that an outsourcing company should be able to address without stuttering:

- What makes up the individual components of an outsourcing solution? Can we see a list?
- How many individuals have been trained in the individual components?
- How long have those individuals been with the organization?

What you will find is that outsourcing companies do not always use the cutting-edge solution (i.e., Gartner/Forrester leadership quadrant products) but rather a knock-off solution. This is to save on licensing cost. As long as the knock-off solution provider has a solid business and the solution is robust enough, this is OK. The risk is that if the business of the solution vendor is not solid, you might have to accept the next knock-off solution two years later, since the first vendor is no longer in business.

Dedicated Resources or Not?

Another aspect of outsourcing that needs to be understood is that most of the time you will not have dedicated resources for all services provided. The business model that most outsourcing companies have adopted requires that resources are always fully utilized and sometimes even over-allocated. Unfortunately some outsourcing companies have a tendency to underbid significantly, resulting in a shortage of dedicated resources and not being able to support all security and compliance requirements of that one engagement. Usually what happens then is that resources start wearing multiple hats—a problem when it comes to segregation of duties. Here is a real-life example: an analyst who was tasked to establish access for the users on the customer side is also the "independent" verifier who is tasked to check if access was correctly granted according to the approved access request. These two roles should be strictly separated from each other. Particularly when you are required to be compliant with Sarbanes–Oxley or any other regulation, the shortage of resources is very likely to create a target-rich environment for auditor teams coming through.

The same holds true for IT equipment. You might have some dedicated resources to your service; however, a majority of the IT resources are very likely shared (e.g., firewall, routers) even in non-cloud environments.

Talking with Existing Clients

Most of the large outsourcing companies will provide you with references. Those references are usually the ones that have reached a stable phase of their outsourcing activities. Those are exactly the ones you do not want to talk to. You want the ones that had problems, that potentially did not go through with the outsourcing decision. As always in life, you can learn the most from mistakes—it is even better if they were made by others. From a smooth-running project you only get the impression that you have made the right decision. So try to get the contacts of organizations where outsourcing activities have not gone that well. No matter which outsourcing company you go with, you will have a higher or lower number of engagements that went wrong or still are going wrong. If problems do not get addressed, this is a clear sign of a lack of capabilities or maturity on the outsourcing company's side. Make sure that you talk with companies that have comparable size, technology, and process maturity level. If business process outsourcing is also part of the scope of your outsourcing initiative then it would be advisable to also get some pointers on how the outsourcing company handled that area.

What Matters for the Outsourcing Company?

The key to success of any business relationship is to understand what is and what is not important for the business partner. Where can I push, where do I need to go another route, and where do I need to give? Unfortunately, most business negotiations are far from having open communication. So to at least understand the business model that most outsourcing companies have in place might help you find those areas where you can push and others where the outsourcing company will not be able to accommodate you. Nowadays in the area of cloud computing, margins for outsourcing companies are slim. They might have a lot of business but not necessarily the margins, and competition is fierce.

There are three basic principles that most outsourcing companies have to operate with:

> *Bring down cost*—Initial investments and operational costs need to be brought down to achieve the margins that are targeted. This is achieved through bringing down labor costs. (Personnel are usually recruited in emerging countries or sometimes in rural areas that have low labor rates. India and the Philippines are just two countries that are often in the mix, but nowadays countries like Egypt are also part of the mix, maybe not as primary service providers but as secondary, i.e., help desk service, to the main, e.g., Indian, staff.)
>
> *Operate within acceptable business risk*—This is a general principal all organizations operate by; however, for the outsourcing company this is especially important because many organizations are putting more responsibility for their business in the outsourcing company's hands. The aspect of liability is something not well understood by either side, each struggling to limit their liability and responsibility in case of an incident. This situation can quickly create business risks that the outsourcing company would not be able to address. For this reason, most outsourcing agreements clearly spell out the limits of responsibilities of the outsourcing company. Those limitations can be the availability of the public cloud (At the time of this writing, for example, one major cloud provider does not count any outages below 5 minutes against their uptime SLA). Another example can be the right to audit, which some

large outsourcing companies do not grant and rather replace it with the offer to provide a SAS-70 or the newer SSAE 16 report. The problem with those reports is that the outsourcing company provides the scope of the assessment. The internal process of granting access at the outsourcing company might be assessed; however, whether staff of the outsourcing company follows your organization's process for granting access is a whole different assessment.

Profit is mainly driven by more customers/work—Margins in the outsourcing industry are much lower than, for example, in consulting. This requires the outsourcing companies to strive to gain more customers to increase their revenue and the profit that goes along with it. This directly ties back to the first principle, bring down cost. Any specialization to the needs of a more "exotic" customer might result in lower margins. Wherever possible, outsourcing companies want to go with standard offerings allowing them to reuse it with other customers. Any specialization will have a high (compared with standardized services) price tag.

Challenges Outsourcing Companies Face

For many people outsourcing companies present themselves as the master of all trades, bringing knowledge to the table that will provide for superior results than what the client organization has ever seen before, bundled with cost savings. This expertise stems from other engagements in the same industry or at least with a comparable IT landscape or regulation. The picture painted is far from reality. In reality an engagement might have individuals that have gained the knowledge and expertise; however, most of the time this other engagement is still ongoing, and the individuals with the knowledge and experience are tied up. This situation gets worse since most outsourcing companies treat each outsourcing contract as a separate microcosm that needs to be cash-flow positive. This is a common approach to manage risk in the outsourcing industry. This setup results in resources (i.e., knowledge) hardly being shared across outsourcing engagements. Even worse, if an outsourcing deal comes to an end, personnel that cannot be immediately reallocated to another engagement are laid off, losing expertise and knowledge. There might be a framework that gets developed once in a while; however, looking across the industry verticals, outsourcing companies are simply overwhelmed with the number of security requirements and regulations that clients have. Knowing this can help you to determine which staff of your organization needs to stay, keeping a good handle on compliance and security.

Which Security Controls—Ours or Theirs?

The answer to this question is, it really depends. What does it depend on? The structure of the outsourcing deal is the major factor. The two extreme cases are (1) an organization stays in their building, continues to use their own equipment, and has outsourcing personnel take over the tasks, and (2) a company decides to give everything to an outsourcing company, which then uses their own staff, in their building with their equipment to provide the service to the company. Those are the two extremes cases. In between those there are many other scenarios that you could be faced with. As a general rule of thumb, the more is changed to the outsourcing way of doing, the more it makes sense to adopt the controls that the outsourcing company has established and add controls to them as you feel they are required to get to an acceptable risk level.

Staff Augmentation

Let's take a look at the first case. A company just uses outsourcing staff. As your organization has done a thorough identification of the threats and vulnerabilities that are applicable to the business and the way that business is conducted, those controls are very likely the right ones to leave in place. The outsourcing company needs to maintain and execute the same security controls.

Complete Outsourced Operation

The other extreme case is that a company outsources facilities, equipment, and staff. The first thought might be to continue doing what you have done in the past, even though the majority of processes, IT equipment, and support staff are going to be outsourced. The security controls were designed for a location controlled by your company, with employees of your company working in the facilities that house the equipment, which is also owned by your company. Now how does the new setup measure up to the controls that you have in place? The facilities are very likely shared, the individuals supporting your company are employees of the outsourcing company, and the IT equipment is now owned by the outsourcing company and potentially virtualized in a cloud environment. How likely is it that your physical security controls can be met in this new setup? Not very likely. The same holds for processes, equipment, and the outsourcing company's employees; however, a mature outsourcing company is able to offer you a solution that meets your security requirements based on what fits their environment.

The dilemma with many outsourcing companies is that many of them have adopted a mode of operations in which client security requirements are implemented, even in the extreme case that everything is done by the outsourcing company. This is a loss for both sides since risk is very likely not properly addressed and money is not wisely spent on controls that do not address your business risk appropriately. An outsourcing company that can standardize security controls across multiple clients will have cost savings that can be passed on (at least partially) to clients. Unfortunately most outsourcing companies have only a thin layer of basic controls (e.g., physical access to the building) that is shared between clients. A standardization would require a more in-depth understanding of the industry the client belongs to, which is an investment of time and money that an industry with paper thin margins is not willing to make, for obvious reasons.

Cost Savings

To gain better cost savings, you should ask if the outsourcing company has a security architecture and a control framework that can be used to secure your outsourced operation and serves as the foundation for a customized security architecture for your outsourcing operation. Once you have received the architecture and the controls, you will need to determine the delta between your control framework/security architecture and the one from the outsourcing company. This effort can result in quite a bit of savings in the long run and in most cases even a better security posture, depending on the maturity level of the outsourcing company. There is nobody better than the outsourcing company that understands what threats and vulnerabilities are applicable to their business and operation. To address the risks of your newly outsourced operation, you will need to leverage that knowledge and combine it with your specific risk to your business.

Security Controls

Depending on the scale of the outsourcing efforts, security controls need to be adjusted. Having outsourcing company personnel at the client site is one scenario that is often underestimated. The client can be overwhelmed, with not enough space for the outsourcing personnel to sit down, not enough network capacity, or simply not having international long-distance service. The following are some of the control areas that require your attention.

Physical Controls   One of the most mature type of controls that keep our information and assets protected is physical controls, which have been challenged in today's world. This used to be quite straightforward during medieval times, but even in ancient times it was not flawless. The city of Troy, besieged by the Greeks, is just one example of how (the original) Trojan horse could circumvent the best physical controls.

To illustrate the problem, here is a typical scenario of what companies have in place:

As a contractor I am required to wear a special badge, showing that I am a contractor. With some organizations it is required that I am escorted at all times. Other organizations do not require an escort but do not allow me to enter certain sensitive areas (e.g., the server room) that are tightly controlled by badge readers and cameras. With those two scenarios in mind, imagine the majority of the IT department being outsourced. The existing access classifications and the various control activities do not scale up. Someone monitoring the server room via close-captioned TV (CCTV) would suddenly see the room being occupied frequently by individuals wearing a contractor badge. The next question that might come up is how they entered the room if contractors are not allowed in the server room. Either an exception was given (i.e., access to the server room was added to the badge), or someone of the remaining company staff let them in the server room so the contractor personnel could perform their work. In both cases the original access policies do not allow access to contractors. They need to be adjusted. However, humans also have their weaknesses, even though they have more flexibility in addressing a situation. For example, a security guard that sees the same contractor enter a server room day after day is very likely going to stop checking if the contractor is allowed to access the server room. In the beginning the security guard might require the contractor to show proper authorization to enter the server room, but over time the guard is very likely going to stop performing those checks, assuming that the situation is the same and the contractor is entering the server room as usual. This human weakness puts the company at risk in case the individual has been laid off and could be a disgruntled employee with malicious intention to hurt the out-sourcing company either directly or through a client. Even with all access being revoked, the security guard might not be informed about the situation and think that entering the server room is busi-ness as usual and the contractor just forgot his badge. The process of allowing the contractor in the server room over and over again allowed for habit formation. Habits form slowly, but according to Lally et al.,[*] the average time for a person to reach the "asymptote of automaticity" was 66 days with a range of 18–254 days. This sounds long but it is really not. A contractor who works three months on the engagement and enters the room at least once a day has a high chance that the security guard has formed a habit of letting him in, regardless of being authorized or not.

---

[*] Lally P., C. H. M. van Jaarsveld, H. W. W. Potts, & J. Wardle. "How are hab-its formed: Modeling habit formation in the real world." *European Journal of Social Psychology*. October 2010. 40(6):998–1009.

Understanding the limits of human controls and automated controls is important when part or the majority of an organization is outsourced. Some of those limitations are also applicable to everyday operations of an organization and might or might not get amplified when outsourcing comes into the picture. Put a review of your "human" controls on the list of things that need to be reviewed before day one. Figure 4.2 is a list of physical security controls that provide a starting point for what to review. It lists some of the physical controls and their potential shortcomings during an outsourcing situation. Please do not take this as a complete list. The list of controls was just chosen as an example of controls that require a review and potentially adjustment.

Logical Security Controls   Nowadays most industries are regulated and have to comply with control frameworks (e.g., Control Objectives for Information and Related Technology [COBIT]). A major trend was set when companies like Enron or MCI-Worldcom were caught with accounting practices that overstated their profits and others not appropriately protecting personal information about customers and employees. This resulted at a federal and state level in the US that many new regulations were passed, intending to stop companies from manipulating their finance statements, or in other cases ensure that private information about customers and employees was protected against unauthorized access. Particularly IT was impacted by many new logical controls that were added to the scope of their work. It is certainly another point to add to the checklist of things to address before day one.

Logical controls have become a critical part of the IT infrastructure, being a large cost factor with obvious and hidden costs. For that reason it is critical that the impact of the outsourcing activity on the area of logical controls is well understood. In the following chapters we will go through some of the key concerns that need to be thought through before making a decision to outsource and what type of model might work for a particular organization. Those concerns are mainly derived from a security and privacy perspective (Figure 4.3 should not be considered a complete list). The controls listed are just examples that require a review and potentially adjustments to the outsourcing situation you are facing.

Physical Control (Example)	Description	Shortfall of Control during Outsourcing
Locks with hard keys	Individuals who require access have a hard key	Most hard keys are easily copied at home improvement stores. It is very difficult to ensure that keys are not copied or to even keep an inventory of all keys with changing personnel. The risk of losing a key is very high with a large number of keys in circulation. Also the replacement cost is directly tied to the number of people having access.
Cyberlocks with PIN	Individuals have a PIN that they punch into a cyber lock to enter through a door.	In case of staff leaving, knowing the PIN, the lock needs to be reprogrammed and the PIN distributed to everyone that requires it. It is very easy for a person with access to provide access to a non authorized person, intentionally or unintentionally, by just telling them the PIN.
Security guard	Checks for ID to verify based on an access list of someone is allowed to enter or not.	With human beings there is always the risk of forming habits. A security guard could allow access to a former employee of the outsourcing company, since he thinks it is business as usual. Another source for human error, which actually happens quite often, is an outdated access list which still lists the former employee.
Access badge	Access is provided based on programmed access rights that an electronic badge-reader checks.	The traditional access model that an organization has established might not scale up to outsourcing personnel taking on traditional functions that employees used to have.
Closed-circuit TV	Monitoring and recording of activities in sensitive areas.	During the transition phase large numbers of an outsourcing company's personnel might be seen in sensitive areas, preparing IT equipment for shipment to the outsourcing company's data center. To discover any malicious activity might be difficult during that time.

Figure 4.2 Physical security table.

Logical Control (Example)	Description	Shortfall of Control during Outsourcing
Shared passwords	Shared passwords (e.g., wireless access points)	Particularly with wireless solutions it is difficult to prevent unauthorized access to the network since physical security controls (e.g., walls and doors with locks) have no meaning to radiowaves. A shared password could allow a disgruntled employee to access the corporate wireless from a nearby location.
Hardware Tokens	Hardware Tokens need to be delivered to foreign countries.	It can be a challenge to get Hardware Tokens shipped to India. At least it will take time or cost a lot of money or both.
Virtual private network	VPN solution was scaled to accommodate normal needs of the organization.	The outsourcing company's personnel might use the VPN to access client systems, creating a shortage of licenses or simply a resource problem with the VPN solution in place.
Change in access behavior	Firewall/router or geo-firewall might prevent access from certain locations.	Depending on your security controls in place, an authentication from India might not be allowed due to the geographical region the log-in is performed from.
One-time passwords via mobile	A one-time PIN password is provided through text messaging.	Certain countries monitor text messaging traffic and could intercept the PIN/password. Also the solution in place might not support mobile phones in foreign countries.

Figure 4.3 Logical security table.

Next Step—Clean House

Most organizations probably have at least some outdated technology or processes in place. Those technologies and processes can cost organizations lots of money and are sometimes kept alive only for political reasons. Examples of such reasons are union demands, interdivisional rivalry, or a conservative decision maker. When the time comes to outsource, those become primary candidates for consolidation.

Too many organizations stall when the outsourcing topic comes up. This results in standard maintenance not being performed anymore and just the bare minimum being done to continue to have IT running. More complex outsourcing engagements can sometimes take years to negotiate, resulting in staff morale being low and IT being in bad shape, such as servers running at their maximum capacity or patches not being applied. If you are already in such a downward trend, it is critical to the overall security posture to work against this trend and plan for housecleaning before the outsourcing company takes over. You should still have many of your skilled employees at that time before the outsourcing company has their personnel take on the responsibility with less-experienced personnel. The housecleaning can help you avoid months of painful problem discovery, after the outsourcing company has taken on the operation.

Maturity Level

Many outsourcing companies have achieved ISO 9001 certifications or other certifications that demonstrate their commitment to delivering consistently high quality services to their clients. However, those certifications do not necessarily mean that an outsourcing company is operating as well as it could. Inefficiencies are the biggest enemy of every organization. This is not different for outsourcing organizations. An inefficiency that was a minor problem in a small organization can become a major obstacle when the organization grows. This can be with a business process or at the human resource level by bringing on the wrong talent. An outsourcing organization's maturity level, when it comes to governance, processes, and human resources, is a critical factor in executing its client's commitments, particularly when it comes to security. Some of the outsourcing organizations see security and compliance still as an overhead that they do not properly staff for. Security tasks and responsibilities are assigned to individuals who do not have the proper background in security or privacy. This can result in significant risk to the client, who was under the impression that he received the same or better level of security service than what was in place before the outsourcing took place.

Alignment of Strategies

Does your organization's security strategy align with your IT and ultimately with the overall business strategy? Now is the time for an honest, detailed analysis. If security is in scope of the outsourcing activities, it had better be in shape. Once the outsourcing company has control of delivering security services, it will be much harder to change directions or the service provided. So having the right strategy regarding how security wraps around the IT and the business services/products delivered can save time and money. Be honest and point out disconnects and deficiencies. Different organizations have chosen different approaches of how security is integrated into the organization. Many efforts have been undertaken to synchronize and connect those models. However, at the current time none have reached a maturity level that would allow providing the reader with a recommendation of what is the right approach. The reality might be that there are different approaches that work for different organizations. Below are some questions that can help you determine if your security program does the right things when it comes to defining and executing your security strategy:

- Do you have access to the IT strategy or the business strategy?
- Is security part of the development of the IT strategy?
- Can you tie improvements (e.g., fewer successful social engineering attacks) to investments that you have made (e.g., security awareness training)?
- Do you have defined security needs for IT initiatives that start within the next 6 to 12 months?

Transforming

Some outsourcing companies might make you believe that by just transitioning services or equipment to them it gets better. That is, in most cases, more marketing talk than anything else. Hearing this, the question of transforming or transitioning comes up. Modern organizations have such a complex mesh of business processes that are sometimes so tightly interwoven that it is nearly impossible just to transform security processes by themselves. Security outsourcing has been limited to certain services that are offered, e.g., vulnerability scanning. When transforming major areas of business processes, security processes also need to be included in that transformation with the risk that the new security process does not easily integrate with the remaining legacy security processes, e.g., certain KPI are no longer available. The outsourcing company usually has a huge interest in optimizing processes to bring down the cost associated with them; this is no different from security-related processes. This optimization is not always in the interest of the client, since it sometimes results in elements of a process being lost due to a lack of documentation. Documentation, or to be more precise, accurate and current documentation is one of the key factors to successful outsourcing.

Outsourcing Preparation

The following section provides you with comments and questions which should help you get the thought process going on as to what needs to be addressed before the outsourcing operation can start. The categories used are aligned with ISO 27002. The categories were chosen to allow reuse of information that some organizations might already have gathered from their ISO 27002 implementation exercise. There are other ways to describe your organization's security program. The chosen grouping is only intended to be a framework to structure the various comments and questions your organization should think about when preparing for an outsourcing situation, whether it is BPO or Technology Outsourcing (TO).

Information Security Policy

 Description: Every organization should have an information security policy that is approved by the management, published, and communicated as appropriate to all employees that exist.

The policy should be clear about management's commitment, and it should state the organizational approach to managing information security.

Comments/Questions: The following questions should help to determine if changes need to be made to address the new outsourcing situation:

- Do the policies scale to a third party executing them? If not, then a rewrite is necessary.
- Have they been updated recently or on a regular basis? If they are outdated or not current, they need to be updated.
- Are the policies technology agnostic? If not, you might have to rewrite not only standards but also your security policies. It is best to keep technology to the technical standard level.

Organization of Information Security

Description: Management should demonstrate active support for security measures within the organization. This can be done via clear direction, demonstrated commitment, explicit assignment, and acknowledgment of information security responsibilities. Information security activities should be coordinated by representatives from diverse parts of the organization, with pertinent roles and responsibilities. Those responsibilities for the protection of individual assets and for carrying out specific security processes should be clearly identified and defined. A management authorization process is defined and implemented for any new information processing facility within the organization. The organization has a Confidentiality or Nondisclosure Agreement (NDA) for protection of information clearly defined and regularly reviewed. It should address the requirements to protect the confidential information using legal enforceable terms. Procedures should describe when and by whom relevant authorities such as law enforcement, fire department, etc. should be contacted, and how the incident should be reported. An organization should maintain appropriate contacts with special interest groups or other specialist security forums and professional associations. The organization's approach to managing information security and its implementation is reviewed independently at planned intervals or when major changes to security implementation occur.

Questions: Having read through the above description of what is expected in this category, how would the outsourcing initiative impact the various areas?

- How does a third party operating on behalf of your organization impact the organization of information security?
- Do you have problem areas with the organization of information security? How would those problems complicate the transition to the outsourcing company?

External Parties' Security

Description: Risks to the organization's information and information processing facility, from a process involving external party access, is identified and appropriate control measures are implemented before granting access. All identified security requirements are fulfilled before granting customer access to the organization's information or assets. Any agreement with a third party, involving accessing, processing, communicating, or managing the organization's information or information processing facility, or introducing products or services to an information processing facility, needs to comply with all appropriate security requirements.

Comments: Particularly with large outsourcing engagements the areas above can be impacted by the outsourcing company taking on responsibilities that could impact the neutrality of the processes.

Questions:

- Is the independence of all areas of this category still ensured when the outsourcing company has taken on some of the responsibilities?
- How does the involvement of an outsourcing company impact third-party relationships (e.g., other partners or customers)?

Information Classification Security

Description: Information is classified in terms of its value, legal requirements, sensitivity, and criticality to the organization. Procedures are defined for information labeling and handling, in accordance with the classification scheme adopted by the organization.

Comments: This is another critical area in an outsourcing situation. The outsourcing company will not bring the tribal knowledge that your organization used to determine how to secure certain information (e.g., without proper label).

Questions:

- Do you have an information classification scheme in place? Is it current?
- Are information assets labeled according to the classification?

Prior to Employment Security

Description: Define and document security roles and responsibilities for contractors and third-party users in accordance with the organization's information security policy. Define and communicate roles and responsibilities to job candidates during the pre-employment process. Conduct background verification checks for all candidates for employment, contractors, and third-party users in accordance with the relevant regulations. The checks should include character reference, confirmation of claimed academic and professional qualifications, and independent identity checks. Employees, contractors, and third-party users are required to sign confidentiality or nondisclosure agreements as a part of their initial terms and conditions of the employment contract. The agreements should cover the information security responsibility of the organization and that of the employees, third-party users, and contractors.

Comments: This is another category that is particularly interesting because this is one of the first (security) processes that will need to be executed to bring on the outsourcing company.

Questions:

- Do the processes in place scale up to ensure that the outsourcing company brings only screened skilled personnel to the contract?

During Employment Security

Description: Management requires employees, contractors, and third-party users to apply security in accordance with the established policies and procedures of the organization. Employees of the organization, and where relevant, contractors and third-party users, receive appropriate security awareness training and regular updates in organizational policies and procedures as it pertains to their job function. There is a formal disciplinary process for the employees who have committed a security breach.

Comments: The outsourcing company's personnel should be included in the scope of the processes and standards in this category. Besides the outsourcing company bringing on staff to help transition the operation, your organization also has to deal with layoffs of sometimes longtime employees.

Questions:

- Does management understand the impact of mass layoffs?
- Do they support additional security measures?
- Is the security awareness training suitable for third parties (outsourcing personnel), and is it still usable after the outsourcing transition has been completed?
- In the light of being laid off, does the disciplinary process still work, or are employees without any discipline?

Termination or Change-of-Employment Security

Description: The responsibilities for performing employment termination, or change of employment, are clearly defined and assigned. There is a process in place that ensures all employees, contractors, and third-party users surrender all of the organization's assets in their possession upon termination of their employment, contract, or agreement. Access rights of all employees, contractors, and third-party users to information and information processing facilities will be removed upon termination of their employment, contract, or agreement, or will be adjusted upon change.

Comments: Depending on what is in the scope of the outsourcing activities, processes like termination or transfer might need to be changed to address the new situation.

Questions:

- Is the process of returning company assets impacted by the outsourcing activities?
- Can access rights still be removed when the organization is going through the transition to the outsourcing company?

Secure Areas Security

Description: Physical border security has been implemented at the facility level to protect the information processing services. Entry controls are in place to allow only authorized personnel into various areas within the organization. Rooms that have the information processing service are locked or have lockable cabinets or safes. Physical protection against damage from fire, flood, earthquake, explosion, civil unrest, and other forms of natural or manmade disaster should be designed and applied. Address any potential threat from neighboring premises. Physical protection and guidelines for working in secure areas are designed and implemented. Delivery, loading, and other areas where unauthorized persons may enter the premises are controlled, and information processing facilities are isolated to avoid unauthorized access.

Comments: Outsourcing companies like to show off their business continuity and disaster recovery capabilities in their offshore locations. However, in July 2012 northern India had over 600 million people without electricity. The data center at the offshore location might be still up but the personnel maintaining it might not be able to come to work. This is just one example of how a situation with the outsourced operation can impact the operation of your "new" organization. Another aspect to keep in mind is that when the transition activities start, with many outsourcing personnel running around in your facilities, you will need to have implemented measures to ensure that your physical access security level stays intact. This could be as easy as making a decision to create a new special badge type for outsourcing personnel that has access excluded to areas that are off-limits for outsourcing personnel. Loading docks and other areas that provide access to the premises should have increased security, e.g., additional CCTV monitoring, to ensure that not everything gets transitioned.

Questions:

- In the case of the outsourcing scope including IT collocation or consolidation, do your physical security policies and standards map to the new facilities, do the physical standards need to be adjusted, or are the physical security standards of the outsourcing company sufficient?
- What access rights do outsourcing company personnel require? Do they require quasi-employee access rights?
- Are special measures required to ensure that offices that used to be in physically secure areas are still secure when accessed by the outsourcing company's staff?
- What are new external and environmental impacts at the location hosting the outsourced operation?

Equipment Security

Description: Equipment is protected to reduce the risks from environmental threats and hazards and opportunities for unauthorized access. Equipment is protected from power failures and other disruptions caused by failures in supporting utilities. Multiple feed, an uninterruptible power supply, or a backup generator, are being utilized. Power and telecommunications cable carrying data or supporting information services are protected from interception or damage. Additional security controls are in place for sensitive or critical information. Equipment is correctly maintained to ensure its continued availability and integrity. Equipment is maintained, as per the supplier's recommended service intervals and specifications. Maintenance is carried out only by authorized personnel. Logs are maintained with all suspected or actual faults and all preventive and corrective measures. Appropriate controls are implemented while sending equipment off premises. Equipment is covered by insurance, and the insurance requirements are satisfied. Risks were assessed with regard to any equipment usage outside an organization's premises, and mitigation controls were implemented. Usage of an information processing facility outside the organization has been authorized by the management. All equipment containing storage media is checked to ensure that any sensitive information or licensed software is physically destroyed or securely overwritten prior to disposal or reuse. Controls are in place so that equipment, information, and software are not taken off-site without prior authorization.

Comments: Keep in mind that you have to translate certain security requirements in SLAs. To do this you need to have your metrics right—asking for an unrealistic SLA does not help anyone. Not every server in your organization requires mirroring of data, which is quite expensive and is chosen far too often due to a lack of understanding of how a particular system supports the business (do you have a current business impact analysis [BIA]?)—an expensive default that can easily negate the cost savings of most IT outsourcing deals. Cable security that might have been a more trivial topic for you when operating out of one or potentially a couple of locations now can become an international exercise. In 2008 a number of undersea cable (also referred to as submarine cabling) outages[*] seriously impacted communication in many of the core outsourcing countries, e.g., India. There is not much you can do about the security of such cabling yourself. However, you can ask to see what the contingency plans are if key undersea cables have an outage. If your equipment is old or is very specific, you might be limited in what direction to go with your equipment maintenance. Most outsourcing organizations struggle to provide support for nonstandard equipment—*standard* being the

---

[*] http://news.bbc.co.uk/2/hi/7218008.stm

Windows and UNICES supporting server hardware. If you are using a Tandem or a proprietary mainframe, you might be out of luck with the mainstream outsourcing companies. Some outsourcing companies have specialized in supporting these types of systems. Moving certain platforms to a public cloud environment can be another challenge. The platforms offered by most of the cloud providers do not support platforms beyond i386 type architectures; Windows and Linux are the predominant platforms offered by public cloud providers. This might change in the future, but the standardization on the Intel platform has been a general trend in the industry that even Apple and to a degree Sun (now Oracle) have followed. As a result the support personnel skill sets are usually limited to the Intel technology (e.g., Oracle being the exception, offering SPARC as a platform)

Questions:

- How do your equipment security strategy and concepts translate to what the outsourcing company offers?
- Are business objectives met in the sense of recovery time objective (RTO) and recovery point objective (RPO) times?
- When was the last time you reviewed your existing support equipment to ensure that you can continue through, for example, a power outage?

Maintenance of equipment is another aspect to consider.

- Is your equipment relocated or is it maintained in your data center?
- Do you lease equipment or have you decided to go with a service such as Infrastructure as a Service (IaaS) or Software as a Service (SaaS)?

Other things to consider in this category are

- What happens if there is damage done to your equipment by the outsourcing staff?
- Does the company provide appropriate insurance coverage to pay for the damage?

Operational Procedures and Responsibility Security

Description: Operating procedures are documented, maintained, and available to all users who need it. Procedures are treated as formal documents, and therefore any changes made need management authorization. Changes to information processing facilities and systems are controlled. Duties and areas of responsibility are separated in order to reduce opportunities for unauthorized modification or misuse of information or services. Development and testing facilities are isolated from operational facilities. For example, development and production software should be run on different computers. Necessary development and production networks should be kept separate from each other.

Comments: It cannot be overemphasized that good current documentation is one of the key factors to successful and secure transition of operations to an outsourcing company. The more room for interpretation there is, the more you run the risk that the outsourcing company creates security problems (e.g., segregation of duties) to achieve cost savings.

Questions:
- Are the operational procedures documented so that a third party can understand them and is able to execute them?
- Is your change management process working, documented, and does it scale to support outsourcing personnel?
- One of the common areas of concern is the segregation of duties with services that have been outsourced; how do you want to control this?
- Do you already have areas in the existing organization where you have concerns regarding segregation of duties?

Third-Party Service Delivery Management Security

Description: Measures are taken to ensure that the security controls, service definitions, and delivery levels included in the third-party service delivery agreement are implemented, operated, and maintained by a third party. Services, reports, and records provided by third party are regularly monitored and reviewed. Auditors conduct audits on a regular basis on the above third party's services, reports, and records. Changes to provision of services, including maintaining and improving existing information security policies, procedures, and controls, are managed. This management takes into account criticality of business systems, processes involved, and reassessment of risks.

Comments: If this is an area you have had concerns with in the past, now is the time to fix this. Make sure that all applicable security controls are included in the contract. Retrofitting security controls into an existing contract is usually quite challenging.

Questions:
- How do you monitor controls that third parties are required to implement?
- Does this approach still work for the new organization where outsourcing personnel is potentially in key positions?
- Is the new organization putting outsourcing personnel in charge of monitoring security controls that are executed by the outsourcing company?
- How do you plan to manage changes to the contract with the outsourcing company?
- Are you relying on outsourcing personnel to help manage the contract changes?

System Planning and Acceptance Security

Description: Capacity demands are monitored and projections of future capacity requirements are made to ensure that adequate processing power and storage are available. System acceptance criteria are established for new information systems, upgrades, and new versions. Suitable tests are carried out prior to acceptance.

Comments: If your organization is weak in this area, you will have issues in successfully outsourcing all or parts of your operation.

Questions:
- Does your organization have a robust and scalable capacity/performance monitoring approach in place?

- Can this approach be used to monitor systems outside the company-owned data center?
- If the outsourcing company does its own monitoring, can it be fed into your company's monitoring system?
- How is this performance data used during planning of new systems?
- Can the outsourcing company offer something that is comparable or even better?
- What is the new process for system acceptance, once the outsourcing company has taken on the task of deploying systems?

Protection against Malicious and Mobile Code Security

Description: Detection, prevention, and recovery controls to protect against malicious code and appropriate user awareness procedures were developed and implemented. Only authorized mobile code is used. The configuration ensures that authorized mobile code operates according to security policy. Execution of unauthorized mobile code is prevented.

Comments: One would think that in this millennium malicious code protection is a standard with all organizations. Still there are organizations without any malicious and/or mobile code protection in place.

Questions:
- What are your controls against malicious code?
- Do you have an enterprise-level solution?
- Are there any issues with the existing solution that might be magnified or potentially even prevent a third party (i.e., outsourcing personnel) from using the existing solution outside the corporate network?
- Is the plan to have the outsourcing personnel use their own systems on the corporate network? A risk assessment of the configuration should be conducted.
- How would the use of outsourcing systems on the corporate network impact countermeasures taken to control a computer worm outbreak?
- Is the outsourcing company using mobile code?

- In the case your organization has adopted a "no mobile code policy," is the use of mobile code by the outsourcing company acceptable? Can it be "white listed"?
- What additional security needs to be put in place to address mobile code used by the outsourcing company?

Information Backup Security

Description: Backups of information and software are taken and tested regularly in accordance with the agreed backup policy. All essential information and software can be recovered following a disaster or media failure.

Comments: No matter whether you perform backups in-house or if you have a third party taking care of your backups, this is another critical area. Once you have to deal with a disaster, it is too late to fix an issue with backups or recovery.

Questions:
- Are your backups tested and recoverable?
- When was the last time you tested the restoration from a backup?
- Are you using a backup system that uses an outdated platform or proprietary platform?
- What is the plan when the outsourcing company takes over?
- Are the old backups still recoverable after the outsourcing company takes over?
- Do backups need to be redone?
- Are you in conflict with applicable regulations or laws in case you choose to not transition old backups to the backup system that the outsourcing company uses?

Network Security Management Security

Description: The network is adequately managed and controlled to protect from threats and to maintain security for the systems and applications using the network, including the information in transit. Controls were implemented to ensure the security of the information in networks and the protection of the connected services from threats, such as unauthorized access.

Security features, service levels, and management requirements of all network services are identified and included in any network services agreement. The ability of the network service provider to manage agreed services in a secure way is determined and regularly monitored, and the right to audit is agreed upon.

Comments: Network security is one of the traditional security disciplines that have reached a high maturity level in many regards. The more widespread adoption of IPv6 has been a game changer for some organizations and potentially created a situation where expertise is missing in house, resulting in security vulnerabilities.

Questions:

- What version of IP does your network use?
- Is your network adequately monitored, or do you feel you have gaps?
- What happens if you allow the outsourcing company to put their equipment, e.g., laptops, on your network?
- Does the antivirus protection of those devices work with yours?
- Can your network devices be managed through industry-standard means (e.g., SNMP), or do you have a proprietary solution?
- Can the devices be managed securely; e.g., SNMPv3 is implemented with authentication?
- Are you collecting metrics that can be used to measure against any agreed on SLAs?

Media-Handling Security

Description: Procedures exist for management of removable media, such as tapes, disks, cassettes, memory cards, and reports. All procedures and authorization levels are clearly defined and documented. Media that are no longer required are disposed of securely and safely, as per formal procedures. A procedure exists for handling information storage. These procedures address issues such as information protection from unauthorized disclosure or misuse. System documentation is protected against unauthorized access.

Comments: Particularly media handling is an area that is under-valued in importance in today's world that is living in the tera- and exabyte storage sizes. A loss of a small USB drive can result in a major lawsuit. Modern USB drives can easily fit the names and Social Security numbers of every US citizen.

Questions:

- Do you have formalized processes in place that state how removable media are handled?
- What type of removable media do you have?
- Are you hanging onto outdated technologies (e.g., QIC-80 tapes) because a critical system relies on it?
- Have you defined an exit strategy to replace this outdated technology?
- It will be costly to have the outsourcing company take this over and maintain it. The not-so-costly alternative is to have the outsourcing company transition the backup to a modern solution; however, the cheapest solution is to do it yourself before transitioning it over.
- Have you thought about how media can be securely destroyed?
- What is the current process, and what are the requirements? Are they still valid, or are there new requirements that would require a new process?
- What are the processes for how information is handled? Usually those processes are tightly coupled with physical security and the security zoning of the facility.
- Does the current approach map to what the outsourcing company offers?
- Who is going to ensure that only appropriate individuals with valid access and need can make changes to system documentation, once the outsourcing company has taken over?
- Is the system documentation current?
- What happens if key people are let go and the documentation needs to be updated?

Exchange of Information Security

Description: A formal exchange policy, procedure, and control in place to ensure the protection of information; procedure and control cover using electronic communication facilities for information exchange. Agreements are established concerning exchange of information and software between the organization and external parties. Security content of the agreement reflects the sensitivity of the business information involved. Media containing information are protected against unauthorized access, misuse, or corruption during transportation beyond the organization's physical boundary. Information involved in electronic messaging is well protected. Policies and procedures are developed and enforced to protect information associated with the interconnection of business information systems.

Comments: Before you are sure that this area is properly addressed, you should not even talk with an outsourcing company. If you cannot ensure that the information you share is secure, i.e., that it is only accessible by the people you designate to have access to it, then you have a serious problem. Security starts with the legal framework, policies, processes, and standards that define what information can be shared and how it can be shared, down to the technical safeguards that need to be put in place to ensure that the confidentiality, integrity, and availability of your information stays intact.

Questions:

- Do you have proper exchange agreements in place that allow sharing of the necessary information with the outsourcing company? A nondisclosure agreement is one of the agreements; another one is an agreement on how data is protected or destroyed.
- If media need to be shared, how is this accomplished? This has already been discussed in Chapter 3.
- Can unauthorized access be prevented during transit?
- How is electronic communication secured between your company and the outsourcing company?
- Is e-mail the only form of communication, or is instant messaging (IM) being used, such as developers around the globe working collaboratively together using IM?
- Are your policies and standards for interconnecting business systems scalable enough to address the outsourcing

situation where a system might not be in the boundaries of the company IT network?

Electronic Commerce Services Security

Description: The information involved in electronic commerce passing over the public network is protected from fraudulent activity, contract dispute, and any unauthorized access or modification. Security controls such as application of cryptographic controls are taken into consideration. Electronic commerce arrangements between trading partners require a documented agreement, which commits both parties to the agreed terms of trading, including details of security issues. Information involved in online transactions is protected to prevent incomplete transmission, misrouting, unauthorized message alteration, unauthorized disclosure, unauthorized message duplication, or replay. The integrity of the publicly available information is protected against any unauthorized modification.

Comments: Most organizations nowadays have electronic commerce as part of their business strategy. Ensuring the security of the data, the confidentiality, the integrity, the availability, and the nonrepudiation are the foundation of electronic commerce. To ensure those attributes stay in place after the outsourcing company has taken on the operation of the electronic commerce systems can be a critical element of success of the initiative or even become a question of survival of an organization if the electronic commerce is the main revenue stream. Online transactions nowadays can be checked for geographic locations. Even with the same IP (which is not very likely if you have the outsourcing organization physically move your IT equipment to their data center), you can experience problems with online transactions of trade partners that have those additional safeguards in place.

Questions:
- Have you already collected information about the security of your e-commerce systems (e.g., when do your SSL certificates expire)?

- How do you ensure that your processes (particularly the ones relying on physical safeguards) are still functional after the transition?
- Do you have appropriate processes and safeguards in place that allow you to protect publicly visible information (e.g., your corporate website)?
- How is it ensured that this information can be maintained after transitioning to the outsourcing company (e.g., domain registrations)?

Monitoring Security

Description: Audit logs recording user activities, exceptions, and information security events are produced and kept for an agreed period of time to assist in future investigations and access control monitoring. Appropriate privacy protection measures are considered in audit log maintenance. Procedures are developed and enforced for monitoring system use for the information processing facility. Results of the monitoring activity are reviewed regularly. Log audits and logging mechanisms are well protected against tampering and unauthorized access. System administrator and system operator activities are logged. Logged activities are reviewed on a regular basis. Faults are logged, analyzed, and appropriate action taken. The levels of logging required for individual systems are determined by a risk assessment, taking performance degradation into account. System clocks of all information processing systems within the organization or security domain are synchronized with an agreed accurate time source.

Comments: Since WorldCom's collapse, the number of audits and the details captured in those audits have increased significantly. Most organizations that have been required to be in compliance with one or sometimes multiple regulations have spent quite some time and money on compliance efforts. A company's work to get into compliance can easily be negated if not appropriately reflected in an outsourcing contract, implementing strict controls to ensure the compliance of the outsourcing operation. Any compliance-related issues with the outsourced operation need to be addressed as soon as possible and clearly documented with what the issue is and how it needs to be addressed. Most outsourcing companies operate with paper thin margins, and compliance activities are a primary candidate for cost savings... at least in the short run, till audits show deficiencies and the cost savings (for the outsourcing company) are negated by having to invest in fixing the deficiencies. Do your auditors understand that outsourcing companies function differently from regular organizations, at least when it comes to engagements with a client? Many do, but some smaller auditing companies are challenged with such situations. Most outsourcing companies have their security architecture tailored to support internal standards and policies; they usually do not scale up to support engagements with various clients. This is also true for the data classification. In most cases a client will ask to have their own policies and standards implemented with systems that are now maintained by the outsourcing company's personnel. So where is the problem? The problem is that due to the outsourcing company's executing, processes need to be adopted and standards on the outsourcing company side need to be established to support the client's policies. For example, this can start with physical security since the outsourcing personnel and the outsourced servers are now in a building that is compliant with the outsourcing companies' physical security requirements, not necessarily the client ones. Since those buildings are shared between engagements, this might result in an interesting situation in that one client requires a specific set of physical controls and another client requires a different set. In the worst case, the two sets contradict each other. Most outsourcing companies are real estate poor, meaning real estate is bought when a client deal goes through. Another example is how personnel are brought on or rolled off an engagement. These processes and standards need to be developed for each outsourcing engagement. Unfortunately, this requirement is not well understood by either the outsourcing company or auditors coming from the client side. The auditors follow their template and ask for policies, processes, and standards at an outsourcing company's level. The outsourcing company's staff then provides the outsourcing company's internal policies, processes, and standards to the auditors. Depending on how experienced the auditor is, they might raise the flag and ask for engagement-specific documents; however, most of them are going to check the box that a policy exists and is formally documented after just spending 30 seconds to review the documents. This is not necessarily an indicator of sloppy work but of the complexity that modern organizations are facing in today's world. There is not only one outsourcing company, there are many that large organizations have to deal with. However, it is a sign of not understanding the typical outsourcing setup at an outsourcing company's level.

Questions:

- Are there known compliance issues?
- Is system use monitored?
- How is log information protected?
- Can log information be protected even after the IT operation is outsourced?
- How are administrator and operator logs handled today?
- What needs to be done to ensure that the actions of outsourcing personnel working as administrators or operators are monitored and the audit logs cannot be manipulated by the outsourcing personnel?
- Are system or application faults logged?
- What is the process to analyze for root causes of faults?
- Does the fault analysis process still work after the outsourcing is put in place?
- Are clocks of IT devices synchronized? If you are in just one location, you might have the clocks set to local time. When going with an internationally operating outsourcing company, you might be up for a sweet surprise when reviewing logs for the first time. Try using Coordinated Universal Time (UTC) instead of the local time.

Business Requirement for Access Control Security

Description: An access control policy is developed and reviewed based on the business and security requirements. Logical and physical access controls are taken into consideration in the policy. The users and service providers are given a clear statement of the business requirement to be met by access controls.

Comments: Access control design is driven by the overarching policy and the standards that are supporting the policy. With an outsourcing situation, those standards very likely require adjustments, potentially even the policy itself requires a review and update.

Questions:
- Are your access control policy, processes, and standards up to date?
- Do you review the access policy, processes, and standards on at least an annual basis?
- What is the plan to adjust the access controls when the IT operation is outsourced?
- Are logical and physical aspects covered?
- How are logical and physical controls impacted by the planned outsourcing engagement?
- Are the business requirements addressed in the current solution?
- If the business needs are not met by the current solution, what can be done in conjunction with the outsourcing company to get better alignment? A solution that might have been too expensive might now be in reach through the outsourcing company's volume discounts.

User Access Management Security

Description: There is a formal user registration and deregistration procedure for granting access to all information systems and services. The allocation and use of any privileges in an information system environment are restricted and controlled; i.e., privileges are allocated on a need-to-know basis, with privileges being granted only after a formal authorization process. The allocation and reallocation of passwords are controlled through a formal management process, and users are required to sign a statement to keep the password confidential. A process is in place for the review of user access rights at regular intervals.

Comments: How access is granted will very likely have to change with an outsourcing company having many personnel taking on roles that were traditionally held internally to the organization. References to job titles in the policies or standards might not match anymore when it comes to roles that approve or review access. This is another area of concern that needs to be clearly spelled out in the contract with the outsourcing company. The importance and the level of effort that are required to restructure the actors in the access control processes are easily underestimated and can be the source for many audit findings.

Questions:
- Are there formal policies, standards, and processes that ensure that users are registered and deregistered?
- Are the existing processes and standards scalable enough to address the outsourcing situation?
- How are personnel of the outsourcing company registered or deregistered?
- How are privileges determined and assigned?
- Are the processes for approval and privilege management scalable enough to address the outsourcing situation? The structure of the outsourcing company might not map to the client's organization; titles might be different or job descriptions vary, resulting in existing process documentation not using the right people/title.
- Help desk—Password management is another area at which to take a closer look. Which access needs to be changed? Which access cannot be given to the outsourcing company's personnel?
- What do outsourcing personnel need to contractually abide by?
- What is enforceable when it comes to an incident that involves passwords? Existing forms may be written with only employees in mind.

- Are access rights reviewed on a regular basis, at least annually?
- Is the review process scalable enough that it can be used with the new outsourcing situation?

User Responsibilities Security

Description: There are security practices in place to guide users in selecting and maintaining secure passwords. The users and contractors are made aware of the security requirements and procedures for protecting unattended equipment. A clear desk policy with regard to papers and removable storage media has been adopted. The organization has adopted clear screen policy with regard to information processing facility.

Comments: With the outsourcing activities very likely resulting in new systems and new processes being needed, it is critical to ensure that password safety is still at the right level—i.e., users, regardless of whether they are employees or personnel of the outsourcing company, are required to use strong passwords. If this is an issue at the current point in time, it will just get amplified when the outsourcing company has taken over systems.

Questions:
- Are you doing the right things now? Do you have gaps? See description above.
- How are you planning to ensure that outsourcing personnel follow the same process as employees?
- Do you have an unattended equipment security standard in place that clearly spells out how the workstations and servers are protected (e.g., screen savers turn on after a certain amount of time and require a login to continue users' sessions).
- Can you enforce the unattended equipment security standard also to outsourcing personnel that might use their own equipment?

We already touched on the potential changes in physical security. Those also can easily impact how clean-desk or clean-screen standards need to be implemented.

- Do you have a clean-desk standard?
- Is the clean-desk standard implemented and enforced?
- Does the clean-desk standard scale up to outsourcing personnel being onsite and offsite? (e.g., regular audits by the outsourcing company and auditors)
- How can the clean-screen standard be implemented including outsourcing personnel?

Network Access Control Security

Description: Users are provided with access only to the services that they have been specifically authorized to use. A policy exists that does address concerns relating to networks and network services. Appropriate authentication mechanisms are used to control access by remote users. Automatic equipment identification (where available) is being used as a means to authenticate connections from specific locations and equipment. Physical and logical access to diagnostic ports are securely controlled, for example, protected by a security mechanism. Groups of information services, users, and information systems are segregated on networks. The network that business partners and/or third parties use to access their information system is segregated using perimeter security mechanisms such as firewalls. Consideration is made for segregation of wireless networks from internal and private networks. An access control policy exists which states network connection control for shared networks, especially for those that extend across the organization's boundaries. The access control policy states routing controls are to be implemented for networks. Those routing controls are based on the positive source and destination identification mechanism.

Comments: With more and more companies looking into implementing bring-your-own-device (BYOD), this area becomes not only a challenge for IT, but also for security.

Questions:

- Has your organization already implemented a BYOD/third-party device standard that is supported by a policy that allows the outsourcing company's personnel to access the network that way?

- If there is no BYOD/third-party device standard or supporting policy, can the existing standards, policy, and processes be adopted to allow for outsourcing company's personnel to attach their devices to the organizations network?

Particularly with large outsourcing engagements, it is critical that outsourcing companies bring people onsite to talk and work with your personnel to capture information and knowledge before it walks out the door in the form of a former employee who has either decided to move on or was let go. At the same time you also do not want to provide network access as an "all or nothing" type. Determining which network access is needed for which outsourcing team should be done by experienced personnel and not the outsourcing company that might provide itself more access than it really needs.

- Does your current process allow for limiting access to just the network resources that are required for certain processes (e.g., firewall log review)?
- If such a process exists, does it scale to include the outsourcing company's personnel and their needs to connect, for example, to the outsourcing company's internal systems using a VPN?

Sometimes an outsourcing initiative takes on such a large scale that it is not feasible to maintain a physical building that can house all remaining employees. Many of the remaining employees are being asked to work from home.

- Is the organization prepared for such a shift in how work is performed? Is there a scalable strong authentication model in place?
- Does the remote access solution have enough "horsepower" to support the increased number of remote connections?

Nowadays the bandwidth available to broadband users at home can be quite high, compared to 10 years ago. What was maybe a good remote access solution three years ago might collapse nowadays under just 10 percent more users.

During transition time you will very likely have many more devices on your local network. IDS and IPS solutions might trigger many false positive alerts due to the unusual nature of the network traffic. Network equipment identification can be critical to make sense out of network intrusion detection alarms. If not already in place, now is the time to put a solution in place that scales up to the new situation with outsourcing equipment showing up on the local network.

- Is your equipment's back door (i.e., maintenance/diagnos-
  tic access), secured beyond access being restricted to the
  local network?

It is a common practice that system administrators create back doors to their systems. The fear of a hacker locking out the system administrator has been around for decades and was profitably one of the first measures taken to address a security breach. Outsourcing personnel preparing systems for a transition to their data center might already establish common accounts on your systems. Even after they leave, the access to your network might now span countries or even continents.

- How do you want to segregate this new network? (i.e., outsourced network and the remaining local network at your
  facilities.)

The layered approach you had in place might not work anymore. Keep in mind that the outsourcing company's personnel have now taken on some of the administrative roles, which in most cases means they have the keys to (your!) castle. To use network segregation and maybe exclude some extremely critical systems from being accessible from all outsourcing locations should be considered.

Network connection control and network routing control are two other critical areas that require your attention. Depending on the complexity of the new network that is made up of your LAN and the outsourcing company's LAN (at least a subset of it), you will not get around the introduction of routing protocols and maybe even Network Address Translation (NAT) rules. Everyone who has seen such a network before knows that the network security will become a nightmare due to the complexity of the structure of it. To introduce network connection control might be something to think about; however, if the outsourcing company does not have already this in place, it will very likely become a half-baked solution (on your side) with limited value.

Operating System Access Control Security

Description: The access to operating systems is controlled by a secure log-on procedure. Unique identifiers (user IDs) are provided to every user, such as operators, system administrators, and all other staff including technical. A suitable authentication technique is chosen to substantiate the claimed identity of the user. Generic user accounts are supplied only under exceptional circumstances when there is a clear business need. Additional controls may be necessary to maintain accountability. Password management systems enforce various password controls such as individual password for accountability, enforcment of password changes, storage of passwords in encrypted form, not displaying passwords on screens, etc. Utility programs that might be capable of overriding system and application controls are restricted and tightly controlled. Inactive sessions are shut down after a defined period of inactivity. There are restrictions on connection time for high-risk applications.

Comments: There are many roads that lead to Rome, and this is also true for securing a system or even an organization. I have seen organizations that prefer the fingerprint reader, others prefer passwords, and some prefer hardware tokens to log in to their workstations. So when you get personnel from the outsourcing company onsite that connect to your network, you might see that they are using a different means of authentication to access the outsourcing company's systems that are used to deliver service to your organization. This form of authentication might or might not be in compliance with your policies and standards. If the access methods do not increase your risk level, it would be advisable to adjust your standards. Most people might just say this is an exception and does not require any change of the standard. Once you open up the floodgates of exceptions for a long-term relationship like the one that you have with an outsourcing company, you will easily drown in exceptions, quickly getting to a point where you do not understand your organization's real security posture anymore. Risk assessment results will need to be reviewed for approved exceptions and the ratings adjusted as needed. This approach might work for your internal staff; however, if you have external auditors, you might be up for a long discussion with them. If your policies and standards are not already written in a way to allow for some flexibility, it is easier to adjust the policies and standards than to go the route of many exceptions.

Comments: User IDs and account access are areas that auditors like to pay particular attention to, because they obviously introduce a high risk, if done wrong or not maintained.

Questions:

- Do you have any shared user accounts that are not accounted for?
- Are there generic user accounts without documentation?
- Is there a process to review accounts on a regular basis?

Now is the time to get your user access in order, before some of the tribal knowledge walks out the door. This might happen sooner than later, once people hear that their job is at risk of being outsourced. Other areas to think about are as follows:

- Can your authentication methods be used remotely by outsourcing company personnel?
- Do you use authentication methods that are homegrown, using e.g., old "unsalted hashes" to store passwords? (LinkedIn learned this the hard way in 2012, not using any salted hashes to store passwords.[*])
- Do users need to show up in person to sign up for an account?

Showing up in person to sign up for an account might not work if there is a global delivery model, and personnel of the outsourcing company requiring accounts are in a foreign destination. The same holds if you outsource this function and it is suddenly located in a foreign country. It is not very practical to expect a user to travel abroad to get a user account. A local trusted resource will need to take on the process of verifying the identity of the individuals that request user accounts.

---

[*] http://nakedsecurity.sophos.com/2012/06/06/linkedin-confirms-hack-over-60-of-stolen-passwords-already-cracked/

- Is there an automated password management system in place? This becomes a critical system that you want to pay particular attention to when it comes to documentation and capturing the tribal knowledge that your staff has accumulated over the years.
- Does your organization use system utilities, for example, for the help desk?

When looking at the level of access and the information the outsourcing company personnel potentially could gain access to, the question of trust comes to mind. Does the use of a support tool that can connect to users' PCs and see everything on the screen and hard drive introduce a risk that the organization is not willing to take for senior executives (i.e., this group would have special in-house support)? Some of those tools allow a silent mode where the user is not notified that a remote user is monitoring what they are doing with their PC. There are other aspects to consider when discussing the use of such remote support tools. In some cases they had been used only on the Local Area Network (LAN), and suddenly they are used across Wide Area Networks (WAN). The delay, the potential Network Address Translation (NAT), etc., can all result in a tool that was used for years suddenly not working anymore, at least not from the remote location that the outsourcing company has in place for support.

Other areas that might create new problems are aggressive session time-out settings that simply time out due to network congestion on the WAN, maybe not during normal operation but during special situations—and the first one to two years will be a special situation with some surprises (e.g., network bandwidth problems).

If you have limitations on connection times, you might have to rethink them. Particularly if the outsourcing company has personnel in India, or other offshore locations, you will see activity during times that your local support personnel normally are asleep.

Application and Information Access Control Security

> *Description*: Access to information and application system functions by users and support personnel is restricted in accordance with the defined access control policy. Sensitive systems are

provided with dedicated and isolated computing environment such as running on a dedicated computer, sharing resources only with trusted application systems, etc.

Comments: If you have had problems in the past with who has access to information and how this access is given, then the problem will just increase when adding the outsourcing personnel in the picture. Whatever you currently have in place is tailored to the internal structure of your organization. Titles and roles might factor in on who has to sign off. Role-based access, entitlement-based, discretionary, mandatory, group-based, etc., access control—each of those models will exhibit slightly different problems related to outsourcing personnel requiring access. However, if you outsource the majority of IT, you will very likely have a problem with your existing workflow since now outsourcing personnel are in the roles that used to sign off on the access. For the majority of access that might be OK; for some access you will want to have someone from your organization to sign off and provide oversight to the process. Just to show that the devil is in the details, having a manager from the outsourcing company sign off on access to reports that were created to evaluate the outsourcing company might not be a good idea. If you have systems that contain sensitive information, they very likely require additional security measures such as network segregation by putting them on a separate network and dedicated computing equipment. This usually can be achieved with limited resources when you own your own IT environment. When outsourcing such a system, you very likely have to make compromises or pay a lot of money to the outsourcing company to create a separate environment. The trend of virtualizing systems and the move to the cloud will require you to transform your security controls, so they can be used in a public cloud environment. There are some guidelines and techniques that can help you. Below are some questions and guidance on how to address the transforming of controls, so they can be used in a public cloud environment.

Questions:
- Can the existing security control be implemented in the public cloud?

- If the existing security control cannot be implemented in the public cloud, is there a security control in the public cloud that can be used to address the risk?
- Does the cloud environment introduce new risks that you need to address with additional security controls?
- If you cannot secure the application/system sufficiently, can the system stay in-house and not be put into the cloud?

Mobile Computing and Teleworking Security

Description: A formal policy is in place, and appropriate security measures are adopted to protect against the risk of using mobile computing and communication facilities. Risks such as working in an unprotected environment are taken into account by a mobile computing policy. A policy, operational plan, and procedures are developed and implemented for teleworking activities. Teleworking activity is authorized and controlled by management, ensuring that suitable arrangements are in place for this way of working.

Comments: No other area has changed the traditional network security more than the general trend of the mobile computing with the latest trend being bring-your-own-device (BYOD) that was kicked off in early 2012 due to organizations trying to bring down the costs for mobile devices. This trend has created a nightmare, not only for security, but also for IT. Supporting various platforms and carriers and ensuring that security policies can be applied to the devices have left the IT professionals scratching their heads on how to address this cost-saving measure. Depending on how aggressively your organization picks up such general trends, you might already be in the middle of addressing those issues, have not even started, or have already determined that the cost savings are outweighed by the additional security measures required to address the increased risks introduced by BYOD. With the outsourcing personnel bringing their devices, you just received another group of devices to worry about. Have you thought about the teleworkers in your organization? You might not have any full-time teleworkers; however, you are very likely to have part-time teleworkers, such as the manager who works from home on Fridays. The full-time teleworkers might be the biggest challenge; sometimes far away from any company presence, they might have seen an office maybe once or twice during the years they have been with the company. If those individuals are on the list of jobs that are being outsourced, you better make sure that you understand what corporate assets they have at home before the word goes out that outsourcing is going to impact their jobs. Implementing tracking processes also helps when you have remote outsourcing personnel use your IT assets.

Questions:

- How do you ensure that the right level of physical security is in place with teleworkers?
- Are your existing policies and processes scalable to a level that outsourcing personnel in a foreign country can use the company's IT assets in a secure legal fashion? (i.e., can all software be used in those countries or are there export restrictions in place?)

Security Requirements of Information Systems

Description: Security requirements for new information systems and enhancement of the existing information system specify the requirements for security controls. The security requirements and controls identified reflect the business value of information assets involved and the consequence from failure of security. System requirements for information security and processes for implementing security are integrated in the early stages of information system projects.

Comments: Security requirements reflect the risk appetite and the capabilities of an organization. Coming up with security requirements that are not implementable does not help anyone. Security capabilities that are built as the result of a strategic security roadmap are usually reusable capabilities. When you outsource your IT and maybe all or part of your security capabilities, this whole model will start to shift, i.e., the outsourcing company might offer other solutions that might have been ruled out in the past for various reasons; however, the solution that you currently have in place might not be acceptable to the outsourcing company for various reasons. To come up with a model of what the security architecture could look like after transition can be challenging due to the many moving pieces that a large outsourcing initiative can bring with it. Still it is imperative to get an understanding of how your risk posture is going to change. This can be a time-consuming exercise, and results might not be available when the transitioning starts. It is critical to gain a high level understanding of where there are gaps, and potential overlap. Depending on which outsourcing company you are dealing with, you will see a vendor bias to one vendor or another. It is critical for outsourcing companies to strike strategic partnerships with vendors to achieve further cost savings. To push for a solution that is not part of their strategic portfolio of relationship partners can easily create a difficult situation. When negotiating with the outsourcing company, you should have two things in mind: what is the absolute minimum that I require to come out of these negotiations, and what is the best outcome out of these negotiations. Being inflexible has a price tag that your organization is going to be paying.

Questions:

- Are your standard security requirements up to date (i.e., do they still reflect the current set of security controls)?
- Do your current security controls, which will be the set of security requirements that will be in the contract, still reflect the current thinking on risk acceptance?
- Do you have security requirements and design as part of your System Development Life Cycle (SDLC)?
- Does your SDLC scale up to the new outsourcing situation?

If you have any deficiencies in the above areas, now is the time to review and update the processes, standards, and the documentations that make up the framework for your SDLC. Once the outsourcing activities have started, it will be much more difficult to change them.

Correct Processing in Applications Security

Description: The data input to application systems is validated to ensure that it is correct and appropriate. Validation checks are incorporated into applications to detect any corruption of information through processing errors or deliberate acts. The design and implementation of application level security ensure that the risks of processing failures leading to a loss of integrity are minimized. Requirements for ensuring and protecting message integrity in applications are identified, and appropriate controls identified and implemented. A security risk assessment is being carried out to determine if message integrity is required, and to identify the most appropriate method of implementation. The data output of the application system is validated to ensure that the processing of stored information is correct and appropriate to circumstances.

Comments: When evaluating an outsourcing provider and its capabilities in the software development space, many organizations still measure against what they have been doing in application security, not the latest thinking of how to develop secure applications. Applications have been in the crosshairs of various groups: hacktivists, hackers, foreign governments, etc. with zero-day exploits being developed for vulnerabilities that were just discovered, and your organization might be at least one step behind. The times when the infrastructure was the main target of attackers are long gone. Input validation, output validation, control of internal processing, and message integrity are some areas that make up a large part of what application develops should be worrying about. Application security by itself could easily fill a book. Since the early 2000s many big names (e.g., Carnegie Mellon) have been coming up with approaches for how to better address security in application development.

Questions:
- Is your application development life cycle appropriately addressing security?
- Are you spending a lot of money on having to go back and fix security flaws, after the application failed a final security scan?

- Does the outsourcing company offer a secure development methodology?—It might be a good idea to spend some time understanding what is offered and if it is better than what you have in-house.

Cryptographic Controls Security

Description: The organization has a policy on use of cryptographic controls for protection of information. A key management is in place to support the organization's use of cryptographic techniques, ensuring that cryptographic keys are protected against modification, loss, and destruction. Secret keys and private keys are protected against unauthorized disclosure. Equipments used to generate and store keys are physically protected. The key management system is based on an agreed set of standards, procedures, and secure methods.

Comments: Cryptography is, nowadays, kind of the silver bullet, when it comes to ensuring confidentiality or the integrity of sensitive information. Unfortunately there is a shortage of skilled people who understand key management and encryption standards in the software development community, which sometimes results in solutions that have the devil in the details. A prime example is database encryption that is "sold" as the silver bullet, addressing all encryption requirements. The database encryption becomes pointless in the case of application-based attacks, where the database allows certain user groups to access the data in a transparent fashion, i.e., the information is available in clear text to an attacker of the application that uses the data. Such solutions may address backup security issues but not other security issues. Particularly key management processes and standards should be reviewed to ensure that they still work as intended once processes are executed by personnel from the outsourcing company onsite or potentially even offsite. If you are required to comply with NIST guidelines that require FIPS-140 certified encryption, you might be up for a surprise depending on who you talk to. This requirement in particular, is not well understood by outsourcing companies that do not have a US government practice.

Questions:
- Do you have a clear cryptographic policy that drives your cryptography standards?
- Do those standards scale up to the outsourcing situation?

Security of System Files

Description: Procedures are in place to control installation of software on operational systems. System test data is protected and controlled. Personal information or any sensitive information for testing the operational database is shunned. Strict controls are in place to restrict access to program source libraries.

Comments: If you had problems in the past with how your operational environment is secured from unauthorized code deployments or other down time, now is the time to put together a list of problems. If processes are not defined and/or security controls are missing to ensure that the operational/production environment's integrity stays intact, then moving this to an outsourcing company will just increase the problem. The tribal knowledge that is very likely used to avoid major problems when informally moving code into production is not there with the new personnel. Documenting the process and also implementing the right level of security controls will not only help the outsourcing personnel to do the right thing; it will also ensure that when you get audited the auditors have a good feeling about how your operational environment is protected against intentional or unintentional changes. Testing of new code should never been done with production data. However it is common practice that developers require production data either to fix a certain bug in the code or to simply do their testing. As long as this production data is properly protected, then this practice imposes just a minimal risk. Unfortunately in most of the cases this is not the case; traditionally development environments are way less secure than the production environment. Thumb drives being used to transfer data from one developer machine to another are not unusual. As long as this is done internally by your staff, you kind of have control over it. Once a development team from an outsourcing company takes on the development, the problems might get much bigger. The team might be sitting somewhere halfway around the globe, in a foreign country. The development team is just concerned with fixing a problem, not knowing that they just had downloaded healthcare information about US citizens to their laptop which was specifically spelled out in the outsourcing contract as data that could not leave the United States, might put you in a difficult situation. The situation gets worse when developers are shared between clients of the outsourcing company, potentially using your data for testing with another client's application. All the scenarios described have been observed in outsourced environments, not speaking of the countless thumb drives that have been lost over the years. What applies to data also applies to source code; being shared via thumb drives, it is not unusual that source code is being lost. Another risk with this practice is that developers have the tendency to keep a copy of the code they just developed, so they can reuse it in the future. If you have not invested time and money into securing system files, now is the time before the problems get even bigger due to missing security controls (e.g., Tripwire).

Questions:
- Does your organization have controls in place that prevent unauthorized installations with IT equipment?
- Do these controls scale up to an outsourcing situation?

Security in Development and Support Services

Description: Strict control procedures are in place to control implementation of changes to the information system. These procedures address the need for risk assessment and impact analysis. There is a process in place to review and test business-critical applications for adverse impact on organizational operations or security after the change to operating systems. Modifications to software packages are discouraged and/or limited to necessary changes. There are controls in place to prevent information leakage. Controls such as scanning of outbound media, regular monitoring of personnel and system activities permitted under local legislation, or monitoring resource usage have been implemented. Outsourced software development is supervised and monitored by the organization.

Comments: The change control process is an area that will be stretched to the maximum during the transition time. To have a scalable process that can handle the volume of changes and the kind of changes that outsourcing an IT operation introduces is imperative to the success of the outsourcing initiative.

Questions:

- Has the change control process been documented?
- Is the change control process always followed or are there exceptions (e.g., emergency changes)?
- Does the existing process scale up to include the outsourcing company's services provided to the organization?

Areas of interest are e.g., conference lines, can they been dialed-in from a foreign country, and are the change control meetings at times where locations with different time zones are operating? A call at noon might be the worst thing for locations that are ahead or behind the local time. Other areas are the way changes are distributed. E-mail might work for a limited number of changes; however, for large number of changes you will need to have a commercial change management system that keeps track of the changes and allows participants to review, comment, and approve/deny changes remotely.

As part of the outsourcing deal you might be planning on a technology refresher, which usually means for servers and workstations an upgrade to a new operating system (OS). This can easily result in your organization coming to a screeching halt if done wrong. Even testing in virtual environments is no guarantee that the new OS is not going to cripple critical business applications on the server or workstation. Testing on a server might be even easier than at a workstation, if your organization has a testing environment that really mirrors production. However organizations are usually short on servers in their test environment due to multiple activities taking place at the same time. This results in the interesting situation of one project requiring an exact copy of the production environment to do their testing before deploying to production and another one trying to upgrade the OS and having to test it in the test environment first before going to production.

- What is your organization's stand on changes to software packages?

Depending on your organization's stand, changes to software packages are strictly controlled or limited changes are allowed without being tracked or approved. If you take a more relaxed stand on this topic, it is very likely to backfire on you when the outsourcing company is trying to get a handle on what the standard install is. The outsourcing company requires standardization wherever they can or they will ask you to pay for customized service, i.e., extra work. This is one of those situations that you might consider arguing. However, the nonstandard way to maintain these software packages is more expensive for the outsourcing company. Too many outsourcing deals go bad simply due to the client trying to get the maximum cost savings. Nothing is free. Thinking you can save 50 percent of your last year's operational budget is simply not realistic, particularly if you expect the same level of quality.

- Have you had information leakage problems in the past?

Outsourcing companies have high turnover rates with staff, particularly in less developed countries. This also goes hand in hand with other moral standards compared with, for example, the United States. Something that we might feel is a lie is just a way of saving face in another culture. So taking software code or other valuable information is acceptable in certain cultures. Other cultures consider it as theft of intellectual property (IP). Data loss prevention tools and strict controls with outsourced software development might be required to ensure that your IP does not wind up in the hands of a direct competitor of your organization.

Technical Vulnerability Management Security

Description: Timely information about technical vulnerabilities of information systems is being obtained. The organization's exposure to such vulnerabilities is evaluated and appropriate measures are taken to mitigate the associated risk.

Comments: Software vendors have been overwhelmed with zero-day exploits, meaning the vulnerability becomes public knowledge and at the same time hacker tools become available to exploit the vulnerability. Due to the dependency of vendors like Microsoft, Oracle, or other big software vendors it is nearly impossible for an organization to fix the vulnerability themselves.

Questions:

- How does your organization handle zero-day vulnerabilities or address vulnerabilities in general?

The best you can do is a work-around or turn the vulnerable service/application off until the vendor provides a patch. With browser vulnerabilities making up a majority of discovered vulnerabilities, it is sometimes impossible to implement any work-around.

- How fast can your organization identify vulnerable systems?
- Does your organization have processes in place on how to address such vulnerabilities?
- What is the SLA that the outsourcing company has provided you regarding patching? Is it realistic? Does it address zero-day vulnerability situations?

If your answer is "no" or "unknown" to any of the questions above, you might want to get a better understanding of how the outsourcing company handles such situations, whether they can provide some metrics on how fast they patch, and how they address zero-day exploits/vulnerabilities. Even if the outsourcing company has outstanding metrics when it comes to patching, this is no guarantee that your organization stays secure in the future if the trend of zero-day exploits/vulnerabilities continues. Zero-day vulnerabilities basically render the traditional approach of develop a patch, test it and deploy it useless.

Reporting Information Security Events and Weaknesses Security

Description: Information security events are reported through appropriate management channels as quickly as possible. Appropriate reporting procedure, incident response, and escalation procedure have been developed and implemented. A procedure exists that ensures that all employees of information systems and services are required to note and report any observed or suspected security weakness in the system or services.

Comments: Reporting security events is a critical process that not only drives the remediation efforts to a security event but also allows for collection of metrics that later are used to determine if measures/investments into information security have shown the success that was expected when they were first put in place.

Questions:

- Does your organization's security event monitoring use industry standard technology or is it a homegrown solution?
- If the solution is a homegrown solution, it very likely does not scale up to an outsourcing situation. Are you ready to invest in a new solution?
- Do your processes around security event notification and handling scale up to the new outsourcing situation?
- Does your organization keep track of security events? Is the process scalable enough to accommodate input from a third party's incident management tool? Or is there a manual process required to track this information (e.g., Excel spreadsheet).

Having people proactively reporting security weaknesses is the dream of every security professional that has been tasked with security event management or risk management in general. This requires trained and educated people that can distinguish a security problem from a problem that might not really be security related.

- Does your organization allow for pro-active security weakness reporting?
- If you have this type of reporting established, is this a process that can be expanded to include the outsourcing company's personnel?

Having this type of reporting coming from the outsourcing company side might be seen as an additional service provided, adding cost. It might even result in a formalized risk assessment that is conducted on a regular basis by the outsourcing company. Just to be clear, this type of reporting is not the same as a formalized risk assessment.

Management of Information Security Incidents and Improvements Security

   Description: The organization has given management responsibilities, and procedures were established that ensure quick, effective, and orderly response to information security incidents. Monitoring of systems, alerts, and vulnerabilities are used to detect information security incidents. The objective of information security incident management has been agreed on with management. There is a mechanism in place to identify and quantify the type, volume and costs of information security incidents. Information gained from the evaluation of the past information security incidents is being used to identify recurring or high impact risks. Follow-up actions against a person or organization after an information security incident involve legal actions (either civil or criminal). Evidence relating to the incident is being collected, retained, and presented, to conform to the rules for evidence laid down in the relevant jurisdiction(s). Internal procedures have been developed and followed when collecting and presenting evidence for the purpose of disciplinary action within the organization.
   Comments: For a security organization to function, it is critical that the responsibilities and procedures are clearly understood and addressed by security personnel, management, and employees.
   Questions:
   - Does management responsibilities and procedures support effective and orderly response to information security incidents?
   - Is monitoring of systems, alerts, and vulnerabilities used to detect information security incidents?
   - Is the objective of information security incident management agreed on with the management?
   - How would the outsourcing company be included in the processes and potentially in the decision making?

Handling security incidents is one thing, but to be able to conclude what the root cause was and to identify patterns throughout the security incidents from the year is another thing. Only if you can do the required analysis afterwards can you learn from security incidents.

- Do you have mechanisms in place to identify and quantify the type, volume, and costs of information security incidents?
- Does information gained from the evaluation of the past information security incidents allow you to identify recurring or high impact incidents?
- Do the existing processes scale up for the new outsourcing situation?

The correct collection of evidence is a critical part of any litigation process that might follow a security incident. Only if evidence has been handled appropriately can it be used in court to make a case.

- Has the organization defined any follow-up actions that might involve legal actions in the case of a security incident? Do those actions scale up to include the outsourcing company?
- Is evidence relating to an incident collected and retained to conform to the rules for evidence presented in the relevant jurisdiction(s)?
- Are internal procedures developed and followed when collecting and presenting evidence for the purpose of disciplinary action within the organization? How would this be handled with outsourcing personnel?
- How can the geographically dispersed delivery model of the outsourcing company be addressed in case of the need to collect evidence?

Those are all questions that should be addressed before outsourcing activities start. The outsourcing company will offer a solution to any of your problems in the security incident space. Just keep in mind; you are the expert when it comes to your business. Outsourcing companies usually have a general understanding of security incident management, but they are relying on you to define the specific requirements, to tailor the solution to your needs. This is best done when you have a working solution from which you are allowed to derive requirements.

If your organization has not achieved a working solution, it is difficult to define the right requirements.

Information Security Aspects of Business Continuity Management

Description: A managed process has been put in place that addresses the information security requirements for developing and maintaining business continuity throughout the organization. The process takes into consideration the specific risks that the organization is facing, identifies business critical assets, identifies incident impacts, considers the implementation of additional preventative controls, and supports creating the documents required by the business continuity plans addressing all security requirements. Events that cause interruption to business processes have been identified along with the probability and impact of such interruptions and their consequence for information security. Plans have been developed to maintain and restore business operations, ensure availability of information within the required level in the required time frame, following an interruption or failure to business processes. The plan considers identification and agreement of responsibilities, identification of acceptable loss, implementation of recovery and restoration procedure, documentation of procedure, and regular testing. There is a single business continuity plan for an organization establishing a framework for business continuity plans on a lower level. The framework has been maintained to ensure that all plans are consistent and identify priorities for testing and maintenance. The business continuity plans address the identified information security requirements of the organization. Business continuity plans have been tested regularly to ensure that they are up to date and effective.

Comments: Now with outsourcing coming into the picture, business continuity management can become a more challenging job, not only that you very likely will have to deal with more natural disasters, strikes, and other man-made problems than before, but you also have another layer of management that you have to deal with. The outsourcing company has their own business continuity program, which might or might not address your needs. In any case if you do not have a working business continuity program, it will not magically start working just because you have an outsourcing company providing most of your IT services.

Questions:

- Do you have a managed process in place that addresses the information security requirements for developing and maintaining business continuity throughout the organization?
- Does this process reflect the risks the organization is facing, identify business critical assets, identify incident impacts, and consider the implementation of additional preventative controls in the business continuity plan?
- Does this process scale up to the new outsourcing situation?

It is critical to the business that risk assessments covering business continuity aspects identify actions required to ensure that a functional business continuity plan is in place.

- Have you identified threats that might cause an interruption to critical business processes? Does the likelihood and impact need to be adjusted due to the outsourcing operation?
- Are there any plans for updating the business continuity plans to include the outsourced operation?

Most business continuity plans seem to lack the information security aspect in them. It is understandable that during a crisis the focus has to shift; however, crime does not wait for better days. If criminals see an opportunity, they will act.

- Does the existing business continuity plan address the recovery time objective (RTO) and the recovery point objective (RPO) of outsourced systems? Are those RTO and RPO times part of the set of requirements for the outsourcing operation?
- Does the existing plan identify the responsibilities during a business continuity situation? How will the outsourcing company be integrated in the plan, to ensure that all business critical processes can function?

Organizations should be using business continuity planning frameworks, which help to build and maintain business continuity capabilities.

- Does your organization use a single framework for the business continuity plan?
- Is the framework maintained, and are all plans consistent and identify priorities for testing and maintenance?
- Does the business continuity plan address the required information security requirements?

The best business continuity plan will eventually be outdated. To ensure a working plan, it needs to be regularly tested, maintained, and reassessed. If you have never tested your business continuity plan, it will be difficult to include the outsourced operation and be sure that it is executable.

- Are business continuity plans tested regularly to ensure that they are up to date and executable?
- Are business continuity plan tests tailored to ensure that all members of the recovery team and other relevant staff are aware of the plans and their responsibility for business continuity, information security?
- What is going to change with the team composition once the outsourcing personnel have taken on responsibilities that used to be with your own personnel?

Compliance with Legal Requirements Security

Description: All relevant statutory, regulatory, contractual requirements and organizational approach to meet the requirements have been explicitly defined and documented for each information system and organization. Specific controls and individual responsibilities to meet these requirements have been defined and documented. Procedures to ensure compliance with legislative, regulatory and contractual requirements on the use of material in respect to which there may be intellectual property rights and on the use of proprietary software products have been implemented. Publishing intellectual property rights compliance policy, procedures for acquiring software, policy awareness, maintaining proof of ownership, complying with software terms and conditions have been implemented. Important records of the organization are protected from loss destruction and falsification, in accordance with statutory, regulatory, contractual and business requirement. Consideration is given to possibility of deterioration of media used for storage of records. Data storage systems have been chosen so that required data can be retrieved in an acceptable timeframe and format, depending on requirements to be fulfilled. Data protection and privacy are ensured as per relevant legislation, regulations and if applicable as per the contractual clauses. Use of information processing facilities for any nonbusiness or unauthorized purpose without management approval is treated as improper use of the facility. During log-on a warning message is presented on the computer screen prior to log-on requiring a user to acknowledge the warning and react appropriately to the message on the screen to continue with the log-on process. Legal advice is taken before implementing any monitoring procedures. Cryptographic controls are being used in compliance with all relevant agreements, laws, and regulations.

Comments: If your organization is required to be in compliance with certain laws and regulations, now is the time to identify all applicable laws and regulations. If this has not been done, now is the time to ensure you have a complete understanding of what your requirements are in the compliance space. Changes to laws and regulations need to be monitored and a process implemented that ensures that the outsourced operation can keep up with those new requirements.

Questions:
- Are all relevant statutory, regulatory, contractual requirements and the organizational approach to meet those requirements explicitly defined and documented for each information system and organization?
- Are all controls and individual responsibilities to meet these requirements defined and documented?
- Can the same controls be used with the new outsourcing situation?

Protecting you own intellectual property rights (IPR) is one area of concern; protecting the IPR where you received permission to use it is another. Keeping track of licenses of software copies is probably the most common form of protecting IPR of a third party, and too often organizations fail with this task.

- Do your procedures ensure compliance with legislative, regulatory and contractual requirements on the use of software/ material in respect to intellectual property rights and on the use of proprietary software products?
- Are those procedures formally documented and implemented?
- Do you have controls, such as publishing intellectual property rights compliance policy, procedures for acquiring software, policy awareness, maintaining proof of ownership, complying with software terms and conditions implemented?
- Depending on the type of outsourcing deal, you might want to consider having the outsourcing personnel use your licenses or their own. In any case to establish a scalable processes that helps controlling the licenses you own is required.

Your organizational records require protection, sometimes required by law, sometimes required by common sense to ensure the continuity of the operation of your organization.

- Are important records of the organization protected from loss, destruction and falsification, in accordance with statutory, regulatory, contractual and business requirement?
- Have you considered the possibility of deterioration of media used for storage of records?
- Has your organization chosen data storage systems that allow for the timely retrieval of required data in an acceptable format?

Data protection and privacy of personal information are for the majority of cases regulated by law; the specifics of how they are implemented is usually left to the entities in scope of the privacy or data protection legislation/regulation.

- Does your organization address all legal requirements of the regulations that are applicable to your operations and collecting, storing and/or processing of personal information?

- Does your organization address all legal requirements of the regulations that are applicable to your operations and collecting, storing and/or processing of data?
- Does the existing security/privacy model scale up to the new outsourcing situation?

Depending on what outsourcing model the outsourcing company is proposing (e.g., foreign countries as location for your data), you will have to work with your legal department on determining if this is a feasible model. Even if it is legally feasible, the question comes up regarding how data breaches are handled in that country or what rights the local government has in that country. Many organizations quickly forget that outsourcing companies go to low cost countries that sometimes are less than stable, economically or politically. Certain governments have laws in place that allow them to spy on any communication taking place in their country, even the ones that are encrypted, e.g., Indian government putting pressure on Research in Motion (RIM), the manufacturer of the BlackBerry devices, to provide the encryption keys, so communication to BlackBerrys in India can be eavesdropped on. After 4 years of RIM refusing to hand over the keys, it finally provided a partial solution to the Indian government in August 2012 which allows the Indian government to eavesdrop on any encrypted communication between personal BlackBerry users in India. This solution is not exactly what the Indian government had asked for. The Indian government is actually trying to eavesdrop on corporate communication. Some might think that it is more interested in capturing some of the trade secrets that go back and forth between the corporate BlackBerry users than actually finding information that helps to fight terrorism. Fighting terrorism was actually used as the primary reason by the Indian government when it asked for the encryption keys. Just to be clear: The encryption is actually a feature that is part of the BlackBerry Enterprise Server, used by corporations. Having such a BlackBerry infrastructure is usually a significant investment that most terrorist organizations would shy away from for various reasons. Also each corporation sets its own encryption key, and RIM denies that there are any back doors. This situation shows how your sensitive corporate communication could be exposed to a foreign government, just by having one support engineer in a foreign country with a BlackBerry tied into your organization's BlackBerry Server. As part of your policy framework it should be clear that use of corporate property is subject to approval, if not used as intended by the organization. This is to clearly state what is allowed and what is not. Otherwise, it is nearly impossible to prevent misuse of information processing facilities or equipment. Use of information processing facilities for any nonbusiness or unauthorized purpose without management approval should be treated as improper use of the facility. This might not be a problematic area at the current point in time, even though organizations sometimes would be surprised about what is being done in facilities or with corporate equipment. Now with an outsourcing organization bringing on personnel that might support other clients from your location your organization has to adjust to what is acceptable and legal and what is not.

- Are the current policies and standards worded in a way that they address the new outsourcing situation, or do they need to be adjusted?
- Does your organization have a warning message presented on the computer screen prior to log-on?
- Does a user have to acknowledge the warning and react appropriately to the message on the screen to continue with the log-on process?
- Does your organization get legal advice before implementing any monitoring procedures?

Particularly now that outsourcing personnel potentially are using equipment that belongs to your organization, some of the "safeguards" and terminologies that employees agreed to comply with are no longer in place. This is an area that either needs to be addressed in the contract with the outsourcing company or it needs to become part of the hardware distribution process, a form that clearly states the rules of acceptable behavior that apply to everyone.

There is hardly any organization that does not heavily use cryptography to protect sensitive information, either for confidentiality reasons or to ensure that the integrity of the information is ensured. Some of those crypto algorithms used might be export controlled and cannot be used in foreign countries. Again keep in mind that the model of the outsourcing company might involve one or more foreign countries that support the engagement. Unfortunately outsourcing models are very complex nowadays, meaning there might be a primary location that supports your organization; however the internal help desk for the outsourcing operation in that particular country might be in a country that offers even cheaper labor. Outsourcing companies are constantly trying to save a penny or two. For example, a large outsourcing company has its internal help desk not in India but in Egypt. This makes it interesting since someone from a country that is restricted from receiving the encryption technology suddenly is trying to troubleshoot a problem with it. Even an outsourcing company's personnel who work locally might have to go back to their home country once a year, for example, to extend their visa, taking a laptop with them that was issued by your organization containing sensitive crypto technology on it. Keep in mind, in the end, your organization is responsible for the proper safeguarding of export restricted crypto technology.

- Are your current cryptographic controls used in compliance with all relevant agreements, laws, and regulations?
- Do the controls scale up to address the new situation with the outsourcing company personnel potentially using your equipment?

Information Systems Audit Considerations Security

Description: Audit requirements and activities involving checks on operational systems are carefully planned and agreed on to minimize the risk of disruptions to business process. Audit requirements and scope are agreed on with appropriate management. Access to information system audit tools such as software or data files is protected to prevent any possible misuse or compromise. Information system audit tools are separated from development and operational systems, unless given an appropriate level of additional protection.

Comments: Depending on how regulated your industry or your particular organization is, you will be familiar with information systems audit controls. Audits can be highly disruptive, and the outsourcing company that you picked will need to support those audits. If your audits in the past have created a lot of "noise" in the sense that they were hardly supported, or scope discussions started during the audit, then you might have some homework to do before you can even define what needs to go into the outsourcing contract. Even your internal audit team might have to shift their *modus operandi* from what they were doing to an "outsourcing mode." What does that mean? Auditors usually work off a checklist. They ask for policies, standards, processes, and evidence of what processes or standards are abided with. This might create an interesting situation with the outsourcing company. If the auditor asks for a data classification standard, the outsourcing company will very likely provide the internal standard that is used for the outsourcing company's internal operation; however, it is not very likely applicable to the outsourcing engagement, which contains data of the client organization (what holds for policies, standards and processes also holds for data classification. One needs to be established at the engagement level). This situation creates a crooked picture of what is being done and what is required to be done. The auditors will use the client's organization's data classification and map it to the IT system maintained at the outsourcing organization, to get a proper picture of the security controls and if they have been sufficiently addressed by the outsourcing company. The protection of information system audit tools is another critical area that would need to be addressed. Some of the audit information collected can be quite sensitive, and having it exposed to an unauthorized individual can be like giving away the keys to the castle. Having said that, it should be obvious that your audit systems in the hand of the outsourcing company's personnel creates an awkward situation. If the answers to the questions below already indicate a problem with your current practice, then you should fix those issues before turning over the IT systems that are having the problems.

Questions:

- Has management approved the requirements and scope of an audit?

- Is access to information system audit tools such as software or data files protected to prevent any possible misuse or compromise?
- Are information system audit tools separated from development and operational systems, unless given an appropriate level of additional protection?

Outsourcing Security Readiness Assessment

Now that you know what areas to address, the next step is to determine the outsourcing maturity levels of those areas. The following describes an assessment process that uses a five level scale to rate the maturity of the security areas previously described. The assessment uses four aspects for a final rating.

- **Process Execution**—How is the process executed? Is the process documented and the documentation well maintained? Are skilled resources available?
- **Process Input**—Is the input for the process documented and well understood, or are inputs not defined and the documentation has not been maintained?
- **Process Dependencies**—Are the dependencies for the successful execution of the process understood? Are the skill sets of the personnel understood and documented?
- **Process Output**—Is the output for the process documented and well understood, or is the output not defined and the documentation has not been maintained?

This assessment is not to determine the maturity of a process but if a business process or a technical process can be transitioned to an outsourcing company with the security posture staying intact during and after the transition. Without understanding the four aspects of a process, you will not be able to adjust it to the new outsourcing situation. You might even discover that a process might not require any adjustment. To get a complete view of the overall picture, it is suggested to use a spreadsheet as shown in Figure 4.4. The rating of zero to five has been chosen arbitrarily. A rating of zero to three could also be chosen, depending on how granular the results of the assessment need to be. Color-coding the ratings can help to present the results to upper management.

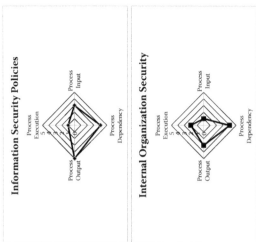

Information Security Policies

Internal Organization Security

Outsourcing Maturity Level Assessment	Process Execution	Process Input	Process Dependency	Process Output
Information Security Policies	1	3	4	5
Internal Organization Security	2	1	4	3
External Parties Security	4	5	5	5
Information Classification Security	4	5	5	5
Prior to employment Security	0	3	4	4
During Employment Security	2	1	4	3
Termination or change of employment Security	4	5	5	5
Secure Areas Security	0	3	4	4
Equipment Security	2	1	4	3
Operational procedures and responsibility Security	0	3	4	4
Third party service delivery management Security	2	1	4	3
System planning and acceptance Security	4	5	5	5
Protection against malicious and mobile code Security	4	5	5	5
Information backup Security	0	3	4	4
Network Security Management Security	2	1	4	3
Media handling Security	0	3	4	4
Exchange of information Security	2	1	4	3
Electronic commerce services Security	4	5	5	5
Monitoring Security	0	3	4	4
Business requirement for access control Security	2	1	4	3
User Access Management Security	4	5	5	5
User Responsibilities Security	4	5	5	5
Network Access Control Security	0	3	4	4
Operating system access control Security	2	1	4	3
Application and Information access control Security	4	5	5	5
Mobile computing and teleworking Security	4	5	5	5
Security requirements of information systems	0	3	4	4
Correct processing in applications Security	2	1	4	3
Cryptographic controls Security	4	5	5	5
Security of system files	0	3	4	4
Security in development and support services	2	1	4	3
Technical vulnerability management Security	0	3	4	4
Reporting information security events and weaknesses Security	2	1	4	3
Management of information security incidents and improvements Security	4	5	5	5
Information security aspects of business continuity management	0	3	4	4
Compliance with legal requirements security	2	1	4	3
Information systems audit considerations security	4	5	5	5

Figure 4.4 Assessment report.

Depending on the time that remains before the outsourcing transition activities start, you might be able to address some or all of the problem areas. Having more areas in "good shape" should result in a smoother transition and a shorter time to come to a normal level of outsourcing operations. Everyone that has gone through a large-scale outsourcing transition can attest that knowledge is the key to a successful transition. Well-documented mature processes are no exception to that rule. Relying on employees who know that they are going to be laid off is usually not a good idea. Between low morale and the time crunch that the outsourcing activities will create, you will find that most "tribal knowledge" is not passed on to the outsourcing organization. By the time you find out that a process is broken due to lack of knowledge, it is usually too late since the employee with the expertise is no longer with the company. Particularly with security heavy processes, this can have a significant impact on the overall security posture. Once the external auditors have taken a closer look at the situation, you will know for sure.

Tactical Goals—Now or Later?

Most organization think that when they outsource part or all of the operations, it might be a good time for the implementation of some of the tactical goals which have been on the book for quite some time. If those goals are still aligned with the overall strategic direction, then they should be included in the scope of the outsourcing initiative. However, an analysis should take place for each of them to check if they are still valid. The strategic decision to outsource by itself might already negate some of them (e.g., better VPN access for IT personnel might no longer be an issue). Examples for tactical goals that make good candidates are security awareness training, management of physical security, access management. If you noticed you have issues with what you currently have in place, then those areas should be evaluated.

Strategic Objectives—When?

Lately there has been a shift in thinking of what makes up the right security measures to allow for the best investment of resources, mitigating high risk areas that are not acceptable to the organization. The traditional approach of the castle with solid walls to keep the bad guys out is long gone. Many corporations have a large number of employees with a mobile workforce using smartphones, laptops and iPads to access corporate systems, reading e-mails, accessing sensitive corporate information from their mobile devices. The next challenge has already arrived in the form of BYOD and the cloud, which has resulted in many cloud-based value-added services, where the sky seems to be the limit. Depending on the agility of your organization's business, the IT and security strategies are being reviewed and updated more than once a year. With this in mind you might run into the issue that an outsourcing company cannot keep up with the requirements that your organization has regarding turn-around time. Outsourcing engagements and the management of them usually adds an additional layer of bureaucracy to the change process. Contracts need to be updated, and legal needs to review them at a minimum. There are examples of large corporations that stated this as a reason to pull back from outsourcing and insource it again. The best example for this is General Electric (GE) a pioneer of outsourcing, which is now bringing its manufacturing back in-house. Another well-known name is General Motors (GM), bringing its whole IT back in-house, after years of having it outsourced. The questions of total cost of ownership (TCO)—sometimes also called Total Cost of Outsourcing—is in most cases underestimated, and particularly the cost for additional security that needs to be put in place to address the outsourcing situation is in most cases not well understood before the outsourcing deal is put in place. The outsourcing company is in most cases not very knowledgeable about a particular regulation that an industry needs to be compliant with. For that reason the approach that is chosen by the outsourcing company to implement the security controls that are required by a regulation are sometimes not implemented as intended by the entity that oversees the regulation. Outsourcing companies are driven by cost and SLA requirements, not by (client) risk. There might be a few exceptions; for example the latest HIPAA ruling (Omnibus[*]) from HHS in the United States clearly states that business associates to a covered entity are required to implement the same security and privacy measures as the covered entity and are as liable as the covered entity in the case of a data breach.

---

[*] http://www.hhs.gov/ocr/privacy/hipaa/administrative/omnibus/index.html

5

DAY ONE AND BEYOND

Day one has come and the outsourcing deal has become a reality. Nothing is free in life, and thinking that you get the same level of quality and knowledge for less money might no longer be a question, but by now you probably already know the answer. Yes, there is always opportunity to save money. However, going with the elusive percentage of savings that some outsourcing organizations present to their customers is simply foolish. You will soon realize that there are other areas you have to invest in, to ensure that your organization can operate smoothly. Sometimes the attitude outsourcing companies take toward risk is not really the same as what your organization would take. The challenge now is to find the right level of control to ensure that your organization gets the service it is entitled to. Even though the outsourcing company holds and processes information that your organization gets from its customers, in the end your organization is still responsible for the security and privacy of that information. A security incident that results in the breach of a regulation might become an expensive exercise for your organization, because it is still responsible for the protection of your customers' data.

You have made it to day one of the outsourcing deal, and the outsourcing personnel have taken over. It is very likely to be a busy day full of surprises, and it will not be the last day full of surprises. Most of the larger outsourcing engagements take one to one and a half years before they can find a normal mode of operations. The time can vary depending on the size of the outsourcing deal or the complexity of service provided. The issues will range from small, requiring slight corrections that are handled informally, to major conflicts in which lawyers put the contract under the magnifying glass to determine what was actually agreed on or, better said, the legal interpretation of what both sides agreed on. Outsourcing companies nowadays operate with very small margins, and asking for something "unreasonable" might become a deal breaker. To see each other as partners or maybe a married couple that is battling life together is more the right attitude. Nobody wants for either partner in the deal to go bankrupt.

In particular, security seems to be something that is not well understood or a primary candidate for cost savings for some of the outsourcing companies. Usually when this is recognized, it is too late and the outsourcing has been in place for a number of months, sometimes years, leaving you exposed for quite some time. Auditors are used to asking a standard set of questions, for example, based on the ISO 27000 series. Unfortunately, standards like that are written for organizations that operate IT as part of conducting a business, and outsourcing IT is not the business itself. As previously discussed (see Chapter 1, Typical Financial Outsourcing Model) most outsourcing companies create separate financial entities with larger outsourcing deals, addressing the business risks of the outsourcing engagement failing. Those entities can still be part of the outsourcing company and sometimes they are separate legal entities that are owned by the outsourcing company. This results in a certain independence that is usually reflected in processes, standards, and policies. The actual outsourcing company's standards and policies usually do not cover e.g., how personal health information needs to be handled, since it is not part of their internal operation. Those new entities now are challenged to either adopt the client's standards or come up with their own standard, which is tailored to the outsourced environment. This can create gaps that are difficult to understand and to discover (if you do not deal with it on a day-to-day basis and just conduct an audit, this might be overlooked). This setup can also result in a situation where the outsourcing company has policies, standards, and processes that cover e.g., financial reports for the outsourcing company. This does not mean that those policies, standards, and processes are being used with your financial data that has been outsourced. This is where the disconnect can happen during an audit, when the auditor asks if the outsourcing company has policies, standards, and processes that are intended for the protection of financial data. The answer to that question is "Yes." However, if the question were more precise and asked for policies, standards, and processes for the client operation, the answer could be "No." It is like buying a car from a manufacturer that has banned smoking in all of its manufacturing plants. You can still smoke in the car. You might not even know that the manufac-turer banned all smoking in all its manufacturing plants. Now, when you are selling the car, you reference the manufacturer's policy of "No smoking allowed." It simply does not reflect what really happened when you owned the car. It is the same with the outsourcing engage-ments. Each of them needs to develop their own set of policies, pro-cedures, and standards that are tailored to address the needs of the client. There are certain connections to the outsourcing company like the reporting of financials, security training, or other requirements that employees of the outsourcing company need to conduct as part of their responsibilities; however, those are in addition to what they need to do to address the client requirements. Here is an example:

The outsourcing company does not have an antifraud training in place. The client is a financial organization that requires that everyone working with the financial systems undergo an antifraud training. The right way to address it is to have the outsourcing personnel that work on the engagement to attend the client's antifraud training. To address this, management of the engagement on the outsourcing company side needs to create a policy that requires outsourcing personnel to attend the training that the client offers on an agreed-upon interval. This is just for outsourcing personnel that serve that particular client and are working with the financial systems of the client. When audi-tors, tasked by the financial client, ask the outsourcing company if they have an antifraud training, the outsourcing company should ref-erence the policy that was put in place for that particular engagement, which requires that outsourcing personnel who access the financial systems of that particular client have to undergo the client-provided training at certain intervals, e.g., once a year. Unfortunately, auditors look at this microcosm the same way they would at a whole organi-zation. This results in policies referenced that are at an outsourcing company corporate level and do not really match up with what the engagement is required to do—to ensure, for example, the security of certain information.

Another example is a bank that decides to outsource its mort-gage business. The bank has an information classification standard that includes "mortgage financial data." The outsourcing company's information classification standard will likely not have this type of information classification in its standard, and even if it does, it is not very likely that the security measures that have been identified by the bank match those that the outsourcing company has identified in its standard. This complexity is often not understood by auditors, and they ask for the information classification standard of the outsourcing company. This might show that contract and financial data of the outsourcing deal are properly secured; however, it does not say anything about the engagement and how it secures the valuable information that the client has provided to them.

Enabling the Outsourcing Company

Now that you have made the step of outsourcing, you need to nurture this business relationship as much as you need to control it. It is critical to enable the outsourcing company so you can get your money's worth. To enable the outsourcing company, you need to understand how they function, what is important to them, and what can create problems for the outsourcing relationship. There is no harm done in trying to get the best for your money; however, nobody gets anything out of it if one of the partners cannot maintain or commit to an acceptable risk level for everyone involved just because the other side insists on shaving off another penny.

Access to Required Information

Having the outsourcing personnel go through a convoluted process that takes months to gain access is not helping anyone. Also getting rid of your old personnel and trying to provide access with the new outsourcing personnel might not result in access that is fully functional and provided in a decent time frame. At least initially, keep your personnel around to enable the new outsourcing personnel by providing access, training, and "tribal" knowledge to them. Some employees might not have an interest to support this; however, if it is possible, this is the best and fastest way to enable outsourcing personnel. Particularly some of the security-related process elements could be transitioned this way; these are often missed in process documents or when reverse engineering a process.

Documentation

If your organization has achieved Capability Maturity Model Integration (CMMI) level 3 or above certified, then I am probably not telling you anything new when I say that good, consistent documentation is one of the key elements of a successful transition to any third party (or after a disaster has hit the organization). Many organizations underestimate this task and have outdated documentation in place. Updating the documentation to have it match the current configuration and setup or process steps is one of the tasks to complete before the transition can even start.

Personnel

No matter how good your documentation is, having a knowledgeable employee who can explain and add to it can be critical to the success of the transition. Keeping a positive spirit among your employees going into an outsourcing situation can save you a lot of money and headaches later. Laying off employees will bring a variety of problems, emotions, and unusual reactions to the situation. Adequate severance pay, assistance in finding a new job, or even asking the outsourcing company to hire those employees can help to keep valuable information available. In most cases they will just move on and find a new opportunity. However, in some cases the individual will react unprofessionally or even aggressively. Since this behavior is very difficult to predict, it is best to take precautions to prepare for the worst case, or at least for some not so typical risk situations, triggered by new threats.

For example, employees with laptops might not return those devices on their last day of employment. Or they might have backups on their own personal computers at home. To address such situations, you need to start thinking about those risks early on. Hopefully your organization already has something in place that helps with the situation and goes beyond just full disk encryption. Full disk encryption with a laptop protects the information stored on the laptop after a theft or if the device was lost, but not when a former authorized user can still use their password to access the information on the laptop. In this case a remote kill-switch or a remote wiping capability is required. This is one of the many scenarios you could be facing. Another aspect to consider is backups. Even with your remote workforce you want to keep this under control. Since the invention of the laptop, this has been a problem; to secure backup for modern laptops with gigabytes of data of employees that spent most of their time on the road. Now with cloud-based backup solutions available, this hopefully changes the way many organizations handle backups (see Chapter 2). Having a user responsible for their own backup can bring various problems with it. A backup drive that is not encrypted and is stored in the user's laptop bag, right next to the laptop with full disk encryption, might defeat the purpose of the full disk encryption. However, the more concerning part is that your organization will lose complete control over the information if you allow personal backup solutions. Corporate data should stay on corporate systems. It is not feasible to expect that the police will search someone's home just because of a suspicion that there might (or might not) be a portable hard drive with sensitive corporate information on it.

Transition Phase

The transition phase will be a difficult time. Employees who suspect that they are going to be laid off or, if lucky, are going to become part of the outsourcing company's team have to work hand in hand with the outsourcing personnel to transition their responsibilities over to the outsourcing company's personnel. This situation might stretch your workplace safety personnel thin, who are trying to ensure the safety of the company's personnel and also of the outsourcing personnel who are on the premises.

During the transition phase the access is going to be transitioned over to the outsourcing company's personnel, and the access that your employees had previously needs to be removed. This is one of the first things that the outsourcing company's personnel need to do, once they feel that they can operate the environment that is outsourced, is to remove access of the client's personnel who are no longer needed. Making sure that back doors are being removed is one of the tasks that you should ask the outsourcing company's security personnel to check for. There have even been cases where employees created problems that they then would fix themselves later on, just to look like the hero and save their jobs.

Access is not limited only to IT systems or applications but also to the facilities. Having a plan that lays out how to effectively revoke access for a large group of employees is necessary. It is advisable to check if this plan really works, before trying to execute it when it is really needed.

Have you thought about the type of badges to provide to the outsourcing company's personnel in the building? Depending on your policies and standards, they might be required to wear subcontractor-level badges. However, is this the right access group? They are going to provide services that might require access to areas of the organization that normally only employees with special clearance had access to. To provide them with a different type of badge that indicates that they are outsourcing company's personnel could help with physical security. It is a bad idea to fall back on an informal model of exceptions such as, "It is Joe from Outsourcing LTD. Let me in, Bob." This ultimately circumvents the physical security policies and standards that were put in place.

The Stable Years

Eventually, if you have not decided to part before, you will have reached a level of maturity in the relationship with the outsourcing company where you feel that things are going well. Service Level Agreements (SLAs) are met; security and privacy requirements are addressed. Now is the time to check to see if the original exit strategy still works: can the organization get out of the outsourcing deal within reasonable time and resources? What needs to be done to bring it back in-house or to another outsourcing company? Particularly in the security and privacy space you can anticipate a number of surprises, having potentially established secure hosting of sensitive corporate information with the current outsourcing company.

Security Incidents

It is likely that there will be security incidents after the outsourcing company has taken on major business processes or technologies. If you suddenly see a sharp drop in security incidents, this can be a good or a bad sign. If this happens, it is a good first step to investigate the contract with the outsourcing company. What exactly is the outsourcing company required to do (1) when they think there is a potential security incident or (2) when they have determined that there is a security incident? These are two very different statements. One requires immediate notification if there is the potential of a security incident; the other one allows the outsourcing company to investigate and determine if the situation is a false positive. The second verbiage might avoid many false positive notifications coming from the outsourcing company. However, it also provides them with the freedom to determine if they have enough information on an incident or not, potentially delaying notification. The outsourcing company might never get to a point that they feel that it is an incident and you may never hear about the situation.

Another aspect of security is the definition of an incident itself. Many contracts do not truly define what makes up a security incident. If the outsourcing company does not use the same definition of *sensitive information* and the contract does not clearly spell out what sensitive information is, the following definition, without any further clarification, allows the outsourcing company to take control: "In case of unauthorized access to sensitive information, the vendor is required to notify company XYZ."

Outsourcing Personnel Turnover

Outsourcing companies usually have a high turnover rate with staff. No matter how stable your company has been, what used to be a small issue when dealing with your own personnel might now be a much larger issue that requires a structured approach. Outsourcing personnel might leave the organization without ever having stepped inside one of their buildings. The model of having personnel work from home, using their broadband Internet connection to shave off another penny of the leasing costs, is not unusual nowadays. However, it creates new risks, such as the retrieval of the corporate laptop from the individual who was only working remotely. It can be days, months, or years before a potential loss of compliance on the client side is discovered—or maybe not at all.

Regular Activities

Some regular security activities should be established to ensure that the outsourcing company continues to provide secure services. Below is a list of activities, which should not be considered complete, that can serve as a starting point. Some activities might be applicable to your outsourcing activities; others might not be applicable.

Access Recertification (Annual)   There are two types of access recertification: the logical access to IT systems and the physical security access. Both should be conducted at least annualy. In the beginning of the outsourcing relationship these reports can be as frequent as every two months. In any case, access recertification should be done at least annually if not more often. The report should contain the name and potentially the personnel number of the individual that has access, what access the individual has, why the access was granted, and who initially approved the access. Usually this could be the supervisor and the owner of the resource; e.g., manager (outsourcing company) and system owner (client) who is recertifying that the access is still needed (outsourcing company or client).

Risk Assessments (Annual)   An initial risk assessment should be conducted at the beginning of the outsourcing relationship, to determine what residual risks have not been addressed and if the residual risk is acceptable to both outsourcing company and client. Once an acceptable residual risk level has been achieved and agreed on, the risk assessment should be updated at least annually to determine if there was any change in risk appetite by either of the two parties. If there is major change (new functionality, platform change, etc.), the risk assessment should be updated to reflect the changes made and the associated risk. Many good risk frameworks are available. One that is free and has been proved to be useful is provided by the National Institute for Standards and Technology (NIST); this is labeled NIST SP 800-30[*] and is constantly updated. Your organization might have its own risk methodology that should be used to conduct the risk assessment.

---

[*] http://csrc.nist.gov/publications/nistpubs/.

Yearly Policy and Standard Review Establishing a yearly review of the engagement-specific policies and standards that the outsourcing company has established is an underestimated task. The engagement specific policies, standards, and processes (as described earlier in this chapter) are required to address the specific environment, data, and services that the outsourcing company is providing to your organization. The outsourcing company's internal policies, standards, and processes will very likely not cover all aspects of the outsourcing operation for your company since their scope is mainly the internal operation of the outsourcing company. With outsourcing companies serving many industry verticals and clients, it would be impossible to come up with a policy and standards framework that could address the security requirements of all clients. It is even more surprising that many auditors that audit an outsourcing engagement ask for policies and standards that have no or only limited applicability to the outsourcing operation for a particular client. For example, the standard for password security that the outsourcing company has in place is limited to accounts on systems that are owned by the outsourcing company. However, the standard is not applicable to a system that was outsourced and is now hosted and maintained by the outsourcing company. To ensure that the system is operating and maintained to client standards, the outsourcing company should establish engagement specific standards and policies that reflect the security requirements that the client has and are adjusted to the outsourcing company's environment (e.g., physical location security and data center security). This won't be a one-to-one copying of the client security standards and policies, since those have been tailored to the client's own environment or situation (e.g., different physical security, location faces different environmental threats).

Those engagement-level policies and standards should be reviewed and updated as needed, or at least on an annual basis.

Good examples for standards and processes that should be established are the following:

- Access request standard for the engagement—What information needs to be provided, who the point of contact is, and how access is provided are just three pieces of information that would need to be identified in the standard.

- Roll-on process—Who needs to be notified, who can approve, and what training is required before the individual can start working?
- Roll-off process—What needs to be done to ensure that the individual's access to sensitive engagement/client data is being revoked are just some of the things to consider including into the process.
- Job-specific security training—What type of training needs to be completed to ensure that individuals who are supporting the engagement do it securely? The annual general security awareness training that most outsourcing companies provide is good but not enough to make outsourcing personnel aware of job specific security tasks that they should execute (e.g., a system administrator will have different challenges than a call center agent).
- Incident response—How are incidents handled, who is notified, and what measures are taken to avoid further damage and secure evidence for a potential legal case?

There are some standards and policies that might be applicable to both the engagement and the outsourcing company's operation/systems (e.g., change management process comes to mind; however, this could follow a hybrid approach based on client and outsourcing company processes). Regardless, if an outsourcing engagement's standards or processes are a hybrid approach (the engagement has to follow both processes, outsourcing company's and client's), an annual review and making changes as needed are critical to a structured operation of your outsourcing activities.

Reporting

By now there should be some well-defined reporting that gives you the assurance that security tasks are executed on a regular basis. In any case it is not a bad idea to once in a while hold a fire drill or create an artificial crisis and see if the reporting really works. For you, the highest priority is your company's secure operation. For the outsourcing company it is providing service to its clients, and you are just one out of many clients that it needs to address its SLAs with. Security does not have the same priority for the outsourcing company as it has for you. You understand the business risk of a failing security control—a risk to your organization. For the outsourcing company this is perceived as a failing SLA.

Daily Notifications   There should not be a daily report; however, daily notifications of security-related events (Note: These are events, not incidents!) should be contractually defined and include the following:

- Information security events that triggered an investigation— What event triggered an investigation? Where does the investigation stand?
- Physical security events that triggered an investigation— What event triggered an investigation? Where does the investigation stand?
- Environmental events that could impact the service delivered by the outsourcing company—These events might or might not have triggered the activation of a Disaster Recovery (DR) or Business Continuity (BC) plan.
- Outages of network or computing equipment that is used to deliver service to the client.

Weekly Reports
- Information security incidents—Listing potential (i.e., false positive) and actual information security incidents for a specific week. What happened, when did it happen, what was done to analyze the situation, and was the client notified within the agreed upon time frame? Those are all questions that need to be answered in the report.
- Changes in processes, policies, standards, or guidelines and why those were changed—in most weeks this is probably not applicable. However, if there is a change, this can serve as a formal notification of the change.
- Staff changes, additions, or attrition (left organization or moved to a new engagement)—This report helps you to track where your equipment went or, even more importantly, if someone still has access to your system and information who should not have it anymore.

- Physical access logs that show which person has accessed the locations and rooms (i.e., offices, computer rooms, LAN closets) that are used by the outsourcing company to deliver service to your organization.
- Physical security incidents that were recorded for locations that are used to deliver service to your organization—When, what, and who was involved with the incident, and what actions were taken? Was information security notified about the incident? If not, why? Was the client notified within the agreed time frame? If not, why?
- Were there any workplace-violence-related incidents?—This might be protected information that the outsourcing company's human resources department is not going to provide. For that reason you should ask to include in the weekly report only whether or not there has been an incident.
- Environmental events like outages of cooling, air-conditioning, power, water, earthquakes, lightning hits, etc. should be included in the weekly report.
- Network or computing outages that occurred and might or might not have resulted in any actions to resolve the outage— What was the root cause for the outage? How was it resolved?

Monthly Reports Monthly reports should summarize the weekly reports, provide some metrics, and show if any general trends are concerning. If there are any general trends that could result in a breach of a security-related SLA in the long run, then this should be indicated. Monthly reports also should provide a summary of security services that were provided during the month. Furthermore, the monthly report should provide an outlook on what is being planned over the next month. Do any activities require the involvement of the client or a third party? This is to alert client security personnel to a potential situation that requires additional measures.

SOC 2 Type II Audit Report This audit report has been discussed in Chapter 4, Understanding What Is Offered subhead, Audit Reports. On a high level, it is a report on controls at a service organization that are relevant to security, availability, processing integrity, confidentiality, or privacy. An independent third party that is accredited to perform SOC 2 audits based on the American Institute of CPAs standard (i.e., AT 101) conducts SOC 2 audits. A Type II report covers management's description of a service organization's system, the suitability of the design, and the operating effectiveness of controls.

The audit report should be reviewed and compared with the risk assessment to determine if the risk assessment, conducted and updated by the outsourcing company, accurately reflects the risks that the audit report spells out.

End-of-Year Security Report   At the end of the year the outsourcing company should provide a report that lists all security incidents, what was done to investigate them, how they were closed out, and who approved the closeout. The report should also contain staff, policy, and standards changes that were made. Depending on your industry you will want to include other information in the report. These reports can serve as a performance indicator. If the reports become longer and longer, this is a sign of a degrading security posture. High staff turnover or a large number of security incidents over multiple reports is a sign of underlying problems on the outsourcing company's side.

Business Continuity and Disaster Recovery Test Reports   Each year the outsourcing company should conduct a BC/DR exercise that is executed based on the scope that you identify. This exercise should be specific to your environment. Most larger outsourcing companies conduct their own BC/DR exercises, however they usually lack the granularity to discover any client specific issues.

6

WHEN WE PART

We are living in a fast-paced world; what was in demand today might not be in demand tomorrow. As organizations reshape themselves, outsourcing needs and existing relationships with outsourcing companies need to change or even come to an end. It might have been difficult to get the outsourcing contract going; however, this is nothing compared with detangling some of the processes and relationships that have been established over the years or sometimes decades with an outsourcing company. Outsourcing deals are reaching a magnitude where new entities come to life due to an outsourcing company's buying part of the client organization to share the business risk. Those deals seem to be "forever." However, no matter how big the deal is, it is advisable to always have an exit strategy that needs to start when contract terms are defined, containing not only the legal and contractual aspects, but also a detailed living technology plan on how to move assets back from an outsourcing company to the organization or from one outsourcing company to another.

Lately (2012) the industry is starting to change directions with outsourcing. Most notably are organizations like General Motors (GM)* that had more than 90 percent of its IT outsourced. The new chief information officer Randy Mott changed the direction for various reasons, but one of the most important factors seems to be the agility and flexibility that comes with one's own IT organization. Mott is planning a major IT transformation at GM, and to be successful he cannot be held back by contracts or the potential inflexibility of an outsourcing company. There might be areas that have created a heavy dependency on the outsourcing company—such as forensic analysis or security incident management and event monitoring (SIEM) that might have introduced proprietary data formats that can only be read by expensive software that the outsourcing company has—but were

---

* Source: http://Informationweek.com/1342/overhaul

199

never an option to be bought by your organization. Regulations and laws might require you to keep certain evidence for a number of years. When ending the outsourcing relationship, the issue of transferring the evidence over to your own organization or potentially another outsourcing company might arise and result in additional cost to you.

Your organization, for whatever reason, might also decide to walk away from outsourcing completely and bring work back internally. This extreme change in direction will let you find out quickly if you have made mistakes during negotiations of the contract or when implementing the processes and standards supporting the outsourcing situation.

How to Prepare

Before an organization can even think about leaving an outsourcing deal, several things need to be considered and certain plans need to be developed and put in place. Some of them need to be put in place even before day one of the outsourcing deal, such as the contractual framework. Others are driven by an analysis of the current state of the outsourcing deal, providing input to the drafting of a plan that defines the changes that will ensure the secure transition of information and systems back to the organization or to another outsourcing company.

The Contract

Every outsourcing contract should not only address how an outsourcing relationship is structured during normal operations, but also needs to define the hand-over to the outsourcing company and the hand-over from the outsourcing company back to your organization or another outsourcing company. Without agreed-on terms every step can become a major exercise. All too often organizations that have decided to outsource think about the good times and the normal mode of operations but forget to define their exit strategy. Putting the requirements, processes, and supporting legal verbiage for the exit in the contract is critical to the successful execution of your exit strategy. Outsourcing contracts without question are complex legal documents that are a challenge for every corporate lawyer to draft or review.

However, it is money wisely spent to have a lawyer with experience in outsourcing to draft and review the contract.

Analysis of What Needs to Be Done

One of the first steps after an organization has decided to leave an outsourcing deal is to review the exit strategy and update it as needed. Does the strategy still hold, or has the organization and/or the relationship with the outsourcing company changed to a level that the exit strategy and the related contractual agreements no longer serve their purpose? If the answer is yes, then this needs to be revisited and necessary changes need to be made sooner rather than later. This will definitely tip off the outsourcing company, and the cooperation might deteriorate. In any case this is the foundation for all of the following steps.

If the strategy and the contractual agreements are still valid, then you can start updating your exit plan.

Exit Plan

The exit plan contains not only technical details but also detailed steps on how information, business processes, and equipment are transitioned back to the organization. This exit plan can be very comprehensive, and this book is not intended to provide instructions on how to create such a plan but rather to point out what security and privacy aspects need to be covered in such a plan. As a general rule, whatever was done during the transition by the outsourcing company can be used as a starting point for the definition of processes that can be used to exit the outsourcing relationship. The exit plan should ensure that the following requirements are addressed:

- At any given point of time, information security and processes ensure the compliance with any applicable law and/or regulation.
- The security and privacy of sensitive information are ensured at any given time of the transition.
- Secure information and system transfer mechanisms, electronically and physically, need to be defined.
- Information is deleted/wiped off any devices that are no longer the official repository of the information.

- Deletion/wiping is done in accordance with any applicable law or regulation. Evidence for following the required process is created and provided to the organization.
- Access to information is at any given time only available to authorized users.

When the Day Comes

So you have the contractual terms in place that allow for your smooth exit. The exit plan has been reviewed, updated, and determined as executable. It is day one of the transition back to your organization. Expect to deal with unusual situations that might not fit into the normal mode of operations during the transition time. You will very likely see security events or incidents, real ones and false alarms. The transfer of information from the outsourcing company's systems to your own systems or the transition from outsourcing personnel to your own personnel will create situations that require additional security that has so far not been in place. Daily security meetings that are used to communicate status and any issues that have been discovered should be established and stay in place till a normal mode of operation is achieved and the move from the outsourcing company back to the organization has been completed. The completion of this move also entails that the organization's information is no longer accessible to any outsourcing personnel. One area that is overlooked many times is the fact that outsourcing personnel, particularly when the outsourcing deal has been in place for many years, become more and more involved in the client's business, which also results in e-mails with client information or other client information being on their laptops, workstations, or mobile devices. To ensure that those devices or services (e.g., e-mail) are wiped or at least cleaned might become a major issue. Particularly Microsoft Outlook, with its way of archiving e-mails to the local file system or in the best case to a shared drive, can create situations where it is impossible to have only client-related e-mails deleted from the devices or archives. To not even allow e-mails to go between the two organizations that are not related to administrative matters of the outsourcing deal might be a good idea. Providing the outsourcing personnel with e-mail accounts on the client side that are backed up to the client organization's backup solution has been one way to address this situation that has quite some potential for information leakage.

Taking Control

Now the day has come and you are no longer depending on an outsourcing company, or maybe you are in a new outsourcing relationship. In any case, you want to make sure that you understand what you got back from the previous outsourcing organization. You could be in for a surprise. Depending on how carefully the contract was worded, the former outsourcing company might not have notified you about certain matters or might not even have executed certain tasks since they were never spelled out in the contract. This happens more often than one would expect. There have been contracts that had the whole security incident part missing.

When you have a better picture of what you inherited, you can create your plan to fix those deficiencies that potentially have created a situation, which requires legal to review the findings and advise senior management on the right course of action. A deficiency that results in your no longer being in compliance with regulations and laws can easily create a huge financial liability for the organization. To then go back to the former outsourcing organization might not be the worst idea but also not the best option. Ultimately your organization needs to be in compliance, and not having checked if the outsourcing company performs the required compliance tasks, is still the responsibility of your organization.

Taking control also means that you need to have the right staff to execute all the tasks that the former outsourcing company performed for you. The next couple of weeks and months will show if this is the case. You might discover that the outsourcing company provided only the bare minimum of documentation or information on how a certain process is executed, particularly if the outsourcing relationship has been ongoing for many years, such things are neglected. Personnel on the outsourcing company side might have executed their tasks but not updated or maintained any documentation that describe in detail what is being done.

Another test that is advisable is to see if systems that came back from the outsourcing company have any intentionally or unintentionally installed "back doors," allowing circumventing regular access mechanisms. This can be management software that is being used by the outsourcing company or a system administrator on the outsourcing side that establishes a back door into the system, allowing them to regain control over a hacked system. This back door checking should be conducted as part of an overall security scan of systems and applications that have come back from the outsourcing environment or maintenance.

Is your network really detached from the outsourcing company's network, or are there still ties between the two networks that potentially could result in unauthorized access from the outsourcing company's side?

Make sure that the contract allows you to fully operate and maintain your systems. If the contract expired or was terminated, did you get all the information that you require to operate? Either way, make sure that you do not wind up in a situation where the outsourcing company is still contractually obligated to deliver a certain service but cannot perform it due to some changes that have been made to accommodate the move back to your organization, or where the systems are still with the outsourcing organization and you cannot get to them because the outsourcing company is no longer obligated to provide access to your organization. These stalemate situations can cripple your operation and are usually not easily resolved, at least not quickly.

Once you have completed the above steps and have addressed all shortcomings, you can finally say that you have regained control over your IT environment's security.

7

Outsourcing Anecdotes

Over the years I have collected a number of interesting anecdotes that show that things can go terribly wrong. Sometimes those things make good material for lessons learned; other times it is material that shows how the complexity of a global delivery model can have a disastrous impact on someone's business. The following anecdotes either have been shared by acquaintances and friends or have been collected from various news sources. Any resemblance to actual people, events, or organizations I have worked with is purely coincidental.

British Health Records

On October 19, 2009, a UK-based TV station, ITV, aired a show with the subject "Health records for sale." In this show ITV revealed a black market for British healthcare information in India. Individuals' health care records were being sold as part of a certain disease group or as individual records. The intimate details discussed between healthcare professionals and patients were available to everyone that was willing to pay enough money for them. This situation triggered the forming of the NHS* Confidentiality campaign. Privacy websites now show patients how they can opt out from having their confidential health information uploaded to the "spine," the national database of patient medical records and personal information in the UK. In this situation the lack of appropriate security and risk management destroyed the idea of having a centralized health record system in the UK, which would have allowed a healthcare provider to gain access to the health information of individuals in case of an emergency. The confidence of the public has been lost and is nearly impossible to restore. This is a prime example of elements pertaining to a national IT system being outsourced without understanding the risk to privacy.

---

* NHS refers to the National Health Service in the UK.

Transportation Strike in Bangalore

On January 21, 2008, a worker in the United States asked the question, "Why is the IT help desk not available?" The answer he got was amazing to him: "There is a transportation strike in Bangalore." Someone might think, why do they not just jump in the car and drive to work? Whoever has been to India knows that the majority of the workers use public transportation, creating a major dependency. Some of the bigger outsourcing companies use their own transportation services, having recognized this dependency as a risk to their business.

On January 20, 2008, the national Indian newspaper *The Hindu* announced a transportation strike in Bangalore, one of the leading locations in India for outsourcing activities. This strike was triggered, according to the newspaper, by dispute over "speed-governing devices" that had to be installed in the vehicles. Even though not all transportation companies participated in the strike, it had a major impact on some of the outsourcing service providers and their customers around the world, because it involved many of the transportation providers. Even providers that were not directly affected by the new regulation joined the group of transportation providers that were—something unseen in capitalistic countries like the United States.

Submarine Cable Cuts

The year 2008 had an unusually high number of submarine cable cuts, cables carrying information between the Middle East, India, and the rest of the world. The disruption at one point in time, according to some experts,* resulted in a 70 percent disruption of Internet connectivity in Egypt and as high as 60 percent for the Indian subcontinent. To varying degrees it also affected other countries like Bahrain, Bangladesh, Kuwait, Pakistan, Saudi Arabia, and United Arab Emirates. Experts estimate that in total more than 80 million Internet users were affected by the outages. Up until today there has not been any evidence of malicious activities that would have resulted in the cable cuts, but it demonstrated how complex outsourcing models are and how many factors play into a smooth operation.

---

* http://www.theguardian.com/business/2008/feb/01/internationalpersonalfinance-business.internet

Cloud Outages

Cloud outages have been ongoing since the first day that someone used the word *cloud*. Some of the bigger outages that happened in 2009–2010 impacted T-Mobile, Google, Intuit, Microsoft, and other big names. The sources for the outages were sometimes simple things that in a traditional operational model could have had minimal impact but had a disastrous impact on the operations of the cloud, due to its monoculture characteristics, where problems easily replicate throughout the whole cloud infrastructure. From 2011 to 2013 cloud outages have become a common thing, impacting large websites. Unfortunately Cloud Service Providers seem to have adopted a practice of not providing any details about outages anymore.

T-Mobile: Sidekick in Danger of the Microsoft Cloud

On October 4, 2009 T-Mobile in the United States experienced a serious outage of their Sidekick service that relies on a cloud provided by Danger, a Microsoft subsidiary. Supposedly an update of Network Attached Storage (NAS) went quite wrong, resulting in a total data loss of some Sidekick users. After six days, without a plan to work it out and no backups in place, some users were left with a total data loss of their contact information.

Outages at Amazon Are Sometimes due to "Gossip"

Amazon had at least five outages between February 2008 and December 2009 that were documented in various news articles. The outages ranged from one hour to almost nine hours, leaving customers of the Simple Storage Service (S3) or the Elastic Computing Cloud (EC2) service without an option but to wait till Amazon had the situation back under control. In one case the company posted an explanation of what had happened. The servers that make up the S3 cloud use a gossip protocol to quickly spread server state information throughout the cloud. At the time the cloud started failing, a large number of servers were spending almost all of their time gossiping, and a disproportionate number of servers failed while gossiping.

Google Services Impacted by Cloud Outages

Google had a total of at least 12 cloud-based outages between June 2008 and September 2009 with Gmail and certain Google Apps being primarily impacted. With over 10 million users and 500,000 business and universities having signed up for fee-based or free Google services, those outages left quite an impression. Particularly the e-mail outages, with e-mail being a fundamental tool to conducting business, had the customers of Google post some nasty comments on blogs. Google still has not released information about the reasons for some of the outages.

Microsoft's Azure and Hotmail

Microsoft's cloud-computing network, Windows Azure, suffered at least one significant outage that lasted close to 24 hours, having users of the Microsoft applications staring at applications that were either stopped or not initializing. Another outage of a Microsoft cloud impacted Hotmail users around the globe. With over 375 million users worldwide, according to Microsoft, this 5-hour outage created quite some frustration. No reasons for the outage were given.

Salesforce.com's Cloud Goes Down

Salesforce.com, one of the leading Software as a Service (SaaS) providers, also had some outages and glitches that could be traced back to processes or technologies failing. On February 11, 2008, some serious performance degradation, resulting in not being able to maintain Service Level Agreements (SLAs), could be traced back to a database utilization problem introduced in a previous release. In another case, approximately 900,000 users of the salesforce.com service could not use the service for at least an hour. No explanation was given for this close to total outage of salesforce.com.

CloudFlare DDoS

CloudFlare has made a name for itself with its role in the mitigation of the distributed denial of service (DDoS) attack against Spamhaus in spring 2013. Everything went according to plan during the Spamhaus intervention. However, in March 2013, CloudFlare came down hard, impacting service for its clients (e.g., Wikileaks). According to the company blog, the Juniper edge router did take a certain filtering rule the wrong way, and the result was that the routers consumed their entire RAM. After approximately one hour the service was backed up, and Juniper was looking into what triggered the behavior.

Background Investigation Lacking

Most of us have not experienced living in a different culture and therefore have not seen firsthand how certain things are handled very differently. Simple background investigations, commonly taking just days or at the most weeks when being hired in Western countries, can sometimes stretch out to months in other cultures. It is not unusual that an unfavorable background investigation concludes three to six months after the individual has been hired—long after the individual has put hands on sensitive customer information. This is not unusual and can happen with large or small outsourcing companies.

Privacy Laws—Not Here

Privacy and how it is applied can vary from one country to the next in the Western world. In some of the leading outsourcing countries it sometimes takes a backseat. Eltasel, a mobile operator in the United Arab Emirates, seemed to have its own idea of privacy and security. According to several reports, Eltasel tried to install malware on its customers' BlackBerrys to snoop on them. It is suspected that Eltasel was serving the local government, but this is still not clear.

Can You Hear Me Now? CDMA Limitations

India is a country that, like the US, uses cell phone technology called Code Division Multiple Access (CDMA), with Verizon being one of the carriers in the United States offering CDMA mobile phone service. On the other hand, carriers like T-Mobile and AT&T use a competing standard that is called Global System for Mobile communication (GSM). Part of the outsourcing deal, which one of largest outsourcing companies put in place, was working from home during off-hours. Each employee working the help desk got a CDMA-based mobile phone to take calls and also to use the same phone for Internet service, connecting to the IT systems of the client. CDMA has just one major disadvantage over GSM (AT&T customers might remember the commercials): you cannot talk on the phone and use the Internet at the same time. As a result, the agents had to hang up on customers to be able to connect to the network with the phone.

Overlooked

After investigating a security incident involving a missing external hard drive that had not been returned by a former employee, the decision was made to not notify the client about the incident. Why? During a contract revision the incident notification clause was dropped in the latest version of the contract. For that reason, the outsourcing company did not have any obligation to notify the client about the loss of the laptop that potentially contained sensitive client information.

Premature Transformation

The client agreed to switch his network security monitoring company. During the transition the new network-monitoring company took on the monitoring of the various Network Intrusion Detection Systems (NIDS). After two months, the client got suspicious since no alerts had been received from the vendor. The client started running attacks on its own network, to see if the outsourcing company was picking up the attacks. The outsourcing Security Operation Center (SOC) picked up none of the attacks. An analysis showed that the security-monitoring vendor could not read certain log formats and had prematurely agreed to implement the solution.

Public Instant Messenger—Share the Joy

A very large outsourcing engagement had many senior executives of an outsourcing company onsite with a client. Those executives were using the client network to connect to the Internet, using e-mail and instant messenger (IM) software to communicate with other executives of the outsourcing company throughout the world. One day the client mentioned that they also had to turn over the IM monitoring tool, which was still monitored by client personnel. All IM communication on the client network had been recorded by the IM monitoring tool. The executives of the outsourcing company had used IM discussing some sensitive details of new deals and current negotiations with the client. None of them were aware that the client had to be compliant with SEC 17a-3, requiring that records are created and kept for communication (including IM) that takes place on the client network.

Index